The Secret of Sweet Treats Kingdom

The Board Game Chronicles
Book 1

Kim Davis

The Secret of Sweet Treats Kingdom
The Board Game Chronicles, Book 1
By Kim Davis
Published by TouchPoint Press
www.touchpointpress.com

Copyright © 2024 Kim Davis
All rights reserved.

Paperback ISBN: 978-1-956851-71-7

This is a work of fiction. Names, places, characters, and events are fictitious. Any similarities to actual events and persons, living or dead, are purely coincidental. Any trademarks, service marks, product names, or named features are assumed to be the property of their respective owners and are used only for reference. If any of these terms are used, no endorsement is implied. Except for review purposes, the reproduction of this book, in whole or part, electronically or mechanically, constitutes a copyright violation. Address permissions and review inquiries to media@touchpointpress.com.

Editor: Elizabeth Constantineau
Cover Design: Sheri Williams
Cover Images: Shutterstock and Adobe Stock

First Edition

Printed in the United States of America.

For my dear granddaughter, Emory.
Without your inspiration, this book wouldn't exist.

In memoriam of Dawn Dawdle, literary agent
extraordinaire. She was a true champion of authors
and gave us the faith to believe in ourselves.
She is greatly missed.

Sofia,

Wishing you a lifetime of adventures and sweet treats!

Kim Davis

So I'm
wishing you a Christmas
and a happy and
a Happy New
Year
Love Dad

Chapter 1

"I win again. Na-na-na-na-na." My little sister did a victory dance as she chanted. Her pink shoes flashed little lights with each step. "I wanna play more."

"No way, Ava. You're a cheater." I swept my arm across the game board and flung the small colorful pieces and cards onto the carpet, where we'd been sitting. How could a kindergartner beat me at Sweet Treats five times in a row?

"Am not." Ava put her face close to mine, shook her long blonde hair, and made the L sign with her thumb and index finger on her forehead. "You're just a loser, Amber."

She had learned some bad things since starting school almost two months ago.

"I don't want to play baby games with you anymore."

"I'll tell Mom you're being mean to me." Ava's babyish singsong voice made me even madder. "She won't pay you for watching me."

Yep, she was definitely learning some bad habits. And I needed the money so I could buy the new voice-activated locking diary I'd seen at the mall. I was tired of Ava breaking into my diaries and scribbling in them. I couldn't figure out how she found my keys or why my pesky sister wouldn't leave my things alone.

"Fine." I crossed my arms and glared at her. "But stop cheating."

Five minutes later, the shrimp was doing another victory dance, shoving her butt into my face. Hot pink flowered PJs danced in front of my eyes before I pushed her away.

"Stop it, shrimp!"

Ava hated to be called that, but she was making me mad. And I had been mad to start with for having to babysit her. It was all her fault I was missing the slumber party of the year. My best friend, Jada, was turning twelve, and I wasn't there. "Go play with your dolls and leave me alone."

Ava stuck her tongue out at me before moving the board pieces back to the start. "Give me your Skittles or I'll tell Dad you won't play with me."

She really wasn't playing fair now. She knew he'd take her side and I'd be the one to catch the blame. Dad was Ava's father but not mine. He adopted me when I was three, right after he married my mom. He tried to treat us equally, but I could tell he loved Ava more. You only had to catch the goofy looks he gave her when he thought no one was looking.

My biological father, which was what my mom called

him, took off before I was born. I'd never met him and only recently I found out his name was Matteo. Mom wouldn't tell me his last name but finally admitted he was from Italy. When I turned eighteen, she said I could ask any questions I wanted about him. But that didn't help me right now when I had an irritating five-year-old trying her best to annoy me and get me in trouble with my parents.

"Fine." I threw the Skittles at her. Candy was the treat Mom always left us when I had to babysit.

"Come on Amber, it's your turn already." Ava stuffed the Skittles into her mouth before I could change my mind and take them back.

Why did Mrs. McGurty have to get the flu and leave me stuck here at home with Ava? All the girls in my sixth-grade class were decorating cupcakes about now and dressing up for Paris-themed photo-booth pictures. Jada promised to save me a goodie bag and a piece of her birthday cake, but it didn't make me feel better.

"I said leave me alone." I picked the game board up and threw it at the wall. The board crumbled into little pieces. Must have been made in China.

Ava's blue eyes filled with shiny tears while her lower lip stuck out and started quivering. Great, I wasn't going to get paid for sure and would probably even be grounded.

"I'm sorry, Ava. Please don't tell Mom." I stooped over to hug her, not really sorry I had ruined her game. I hated her Sweet Treats game, but I didn't want to get in trouble. "I'll buy you a new one, okay?"

A rumbling sound filled my ears and the ground started tilting and rolling. The light hanging over the dining room table began swaying and the wood mini-blinds rubbing against the windows sounded like fingernails on a chalkboard.

"Amber?" Ava grabbed my hand and held on tight.

"Don't worry. It's just an earthquake." Growing up in Southern California you got used to this kind of thing. "Remember what they taught you at school? Drop, cover, and hold on?"

I pulled her toward the dining room table to hide beneath it, although I was positive by the time we got into position the quake would be over.

We were ten steps away from the table when Ava stopped walking. She yanked my arm and started pulling me backward, toward the family room. I heard the crash of glass breaking on the kitchen tile and was glad I had flip-flops on. Our family portrait fell from the dining room wall, the glass splintering from the black frame sent shards of glass flying across the room. A small piece caught my ankle, sending a sting up my leg.

"Knock it off, shrimp. We need to get under the table right now!" While I had been in several earthquakes, this felt different. It wasn't slowing or stopping, like I thought it would. I didn't want to admit it, but I was scared. Could this be the "big one" grownups talked about?

Instead of letting me lead her toward the dining table, Ava began pulling me harder toward the family room. With my feet sliding on the slick tile, I couldn't stop.

"What's that?" I had never heard my sister screech like that before, so I turned around to see what she was talking about.

The small fragments of the Sweet Treats board were hovering in midair, swirling in a circle, going faster and faster. The floor tilted us toward the flying pieces, and we were slipping toward the growing whirlwind. The edge of the vortex was expanding outward at a rapid rate, while the center was a dark, black hole. It looked like a giant vacuum hose, and it was sucking us toward it.

My terrified sister started screaming, clinging to my legs. "Do something, Amber!"

I started shrieking as I tripped over Ava, and we were pulled head first into the middle of the vortex.

Chapter 2

Falling into the darkness, Ava and I somehow managed to keep ahold of each other's hand. It wasn't easy since we were being tossed around like ragdolls, upside down, turning around in circles, bouncing off the black rubbery walls of the vortex. Wind howled in my ears as we fell, while Ava and my screams blended together. Then all of a sudden, the wind died, the sound of our shrill voices went quiet, and then there was complete silence. Complete creepy silence since my throat was burning as I continued screaming my head off. Was I going deaf? It was too dark to see if Ava could hear me screaming.

Finally, our fall felt like it was slowing, almost like we were floating with a parachute instead of freefall. I could hear our screams again. We plunged into bright sunlight and immediately started bouncing after landing on something blue and jiggly. Jell-O? The super trampoline looked and smelled like blue raspberry Jell-O! I tried to stop my bouncing so we could make our way off but, with each movement, my feet left the surface, and I pulled Ava into the air with me. Thinking we could hop toward the side didn't work either. The trampoline threw us one way and then another, no matter what direction we tried to go. The surface was enormous, maybe about the size of a football field, and we were right in the middle. This would take a long time to get off. So far Ava hadn't said a word. I think she was trying to keep from being tossed around like a ragdoll every time I bounced.

I finally crossed my legs in front of me, crisscross-applesauce style, so my bottom landed on the Jell-O. This time we didn't bounce so high, but it still took a minute to sit without springing back into the air.

"Are you okay?" I looked her over to make sure she wasn't injured. "You didn't get hurt, did you?"

"I don't think so." Ava's lower lip was quivering, and her cheeks were bright pink, while her baby-blue eyes were threatening to spill over with tears. "Why is the sun shining? It's nighttime at home."

"I don't know, baby." I know, first shrimp and now baby. Shrimp was reserved for when I was really annoyed with her, which was most of the time. Baby was for special moments when I was really glad I had a sister. Like now. "Let's get off this thing and see if we can find out."

"Where are we? How are Mom and Dad going to find

us?" Her little voice squeaked, and shiny liquid rolled down her cheeks. "I think we're lost, and they won't ever find us."

"Don't forget Dad's the best detective in all of Orange County." I gave her a hug. "Remember, he's getting that award tonight? Detective Addison, super hero! If anyone can find us, he can."

I had serious doubts he'd be able to find us, unless that swirling vortex was still open when my parents got home. Somehow, I knew we weren't in Orange County or even California anymore. Hopefully, someone in this strange place could tell us how to find our way home. But I wasn't going to worry Ava about that detail, especially since I had no idea how we got here or where we were.

I rolled over to my hands and knees and crawled toward the side, with Ava beside me. As long as we moved slowly, we didn't bounce too much. The surface of the bouncy thing was slippery, though, and I saw her do a face plant when her hands slid out from beneath her. I was expecting more tears, but instead she giggled.

"You've got to taste this! It's Jell-O, and it's yummy." Ava started licking the bouncing Jell-O.

"Gross! You don't know who or what has been on this thing." I jerked her back onto her hands and knees and pushed her toward the grass.

It was slow going, but we finally made it to the side. Instead of finding green grass, though, it was shredded coconut that had been tinted green. Ava had to eat some as soon as she saw it and smelled the sugar. That kid had a sweet tooth that just wouldn't quit. "You've got to try this. It tastes like the grass Mom makes at Easter for our cupcakes!"

I yanked her onto her feet. "You can't be putting strange things into your mouth. We don't know where we are, and we certainly don't know if this stuff is safe to eat."

"Well, it tastes good." She stuck her tongue out at me.

I glared at her, trying to come up with a smart-alecky remark, but my mind went blank when I smelled mint floating on the breeze. Ava might like all things that are sugar, but I had a weakness for mint, especially mint chocolate chip ice cream.

I started sniffing the air like a dog, trying to find the source when Ava screeched, buried her head in my stomach and wrapped her arms around me.

"Excuse me, miss, I didn't mean to startle you." The man's soft voice had a faint British accent, and the mint smell was even stronger.

I turned around and screeched, sounding like Ava. A giant mint-green rabbit was staring at me.

Chapter 3

"Oh my, I sincerely apologize for startling you, miss." The rabbit swept a black top hat from his head and bowed, his green ears brushing the coconut grass. "Allow me to introduce myself. I am Mister Minty at your service."

He was about my height, just over five feet tall while standing on his hind legs. His fur was a light mint-green color, just like my favorite ice cream, and when he spoke, the smell of mint filled the air. Ava peeked around me, her blue eyes wide. At least she wasn't screaming anymore.

"You're a talking bunny!" She reached out to touch his paw. "And you smell so yummy. Do you taste good too?"

"Ava, mind your manners." My voice sounded sharp in the quiet air.

Mister Minty's whiskers quivered, and his green eyes blinked rapidly before he bowed deeply before Ava. "Your majesty, you're here! The citizens of Sweet Treats Kingdom have long been awaiting your arrival, and it gives me great pleasure to be the first to welcome you to our land."

"What are you talking about? Ava isn't royalty." A royal pain in the butt maybe, but definitely not a princess.

I expected Ava to start cheering or doing her princess wave thing with the minty rabbit's declaration, but she had her face buried in a patch of coconut grass.

"Your Highness." Mister Minty tried getting Ava's attention away from the sugary treat by tapping her shoulder. "Clearly you need to train your maid better. It simply won't do to have your attendant show you such disrespect."

Me? Her maid? An attendant? No way! "For your information, rabbit, I'm Ava's older sister."

People often assumed I was adopted because my skin had an olive tone, I had dark black curly hair, and my eyes were an amber color. I was also tall and a bit chunky for my age. I was sure I got my looks from my biological father. On the other hand, Ava, Mom, and Dad all had light-blond, straight hair, crystal-blue eyes, and were slender. Mom says they had petite frames while I had an athletic build which made me good in soccer and softball. I still felt like a klutz compared to my sister and mother, though.

"Excuse me, Your Highness." Mister Minty directed his full attention to Ava, who was now looking intently at what appeared to be bright-pink rock candy. "How can this be? Our legend only foretold your arrival."

"Legend, what legend?" I wanted answers on where we

were and why Ava was getting the attention.

"A golden child will fall from the clouds and break the evil spell that enslaves our people." He looked me over before wrinkling his nose. "It said nothing about a sister."

I shook my head. "I think you've got Ava confused with some other golden child. She's not a princess, and I don't think it's possible for a five-year-old to break spells. Besides, we don't have spells, either good or bad, back home."

Ava had apparently run out of fascination with the coconut grass and rock candy because I turned around just in time to slap a red flower away from her lips.

"How many times do I have to tell you to not eat anything? We have no idea if it's safe or not." My voice was harsher than I meant but, then again, I was really stressed out.

"But I'm hungry and that was a cherry lollipop." She stared at the shattered flower lying at her feet for a moment then reached for another flower growing along the banks of the Jell-O trampoline. "Right, Mister Minty? It's safe to eat these?"

"Of course, Your Highness. You may eat all you want. However, do keep in mind a banquet will be prepared for you and your, ah, um, sister. The people of our kingdom will want to honor you for coming to their rescue."

"Look, Mister Minty, I'm sure you mean well, but my sister is going to get crazy if she eats too much sugar." I rolled my eyes as Ava tried to stuff three lollipops in her mouth all at once. "She'll be bouncing off the walls or even worse. Is there something besides sugar we can feed her now? Maybe some goldfish or pretzels?"

The rabbit started choking and coughing, and I thought his whiskers were looking a bit yellowish, instead of green. "But this is the kingdom of Sweet Treats. Surely you understand that's all we eat? Besides, how could you consider eating a poor, innocent fish?"

Ava laughed. Not a nice laugh, either. All I could think was the sugar was already making her wild and crazy.

"Silly rabbit! Amber wasn't talking about real fish, but goldfish crackers. Made from cheese and stuff. Are you the Easter Bunny? He always brings me jelly beans. I like jelly beans and lollipops and Peeps. Hey, do you have Peeps here? I like marshmallows too cause I think that's what Peeps are made of. And I like . . ." Ava's voice trailed off when I snatched two new lollipops from her hand.

"And that's why we don't let her eat too much sugar." I pulled Ava away from a new patch of purple lollipop flowers that she was drooling over. "Shrimp, apologize to Mister Minty. It wasn't nice to call him silly."

"No! I won't until you give me another lollipop."

Uh oh, we were heading for a meltdown. I hadn't seen one of those since Dad took Ava to the circus last summer and let her eat cotton candy, an Icee, and ice cream, to top it off. I'd never heard Mom yell at anyone before, but she sure told Dad off after she finally got Ava to sleep around two in the morning. Lots of sugar really didn't agree with my sister.

"Your Highness, I think it's best we start our journey to the castle." Mister Minty frowned and his ears were twitching erratically. "It's not safe to be out here after dark."

I had no idea what he was talking about. How could we be in danger? We were in Sweet Treats Kingdom, after all. "This has been a huge mistake or misunderstanding, Mister Minty. We really and truly aren't princesses. I only want to find our way home before our parents get worried about us."

"Perhaps if you come to the castle with me, the Duke of Custard will know how to get you home." Mister Minty shook his head. "I had such high hopes your golden sister was the answer to our problems."

I placed my hand on the rabbit's paw while tightly holding on to Ava with my other. I didn't need her getting away from me and eating more sugar. "I'm so sorry we can't help, but we'll go with you to see the Duke."

I had my own high hopes that the Duke of Custard would be able to tell us how to find our way home.

Before we could step even one foot onto the pink and purple crushed rock candy road, a white carriage, trimmed with gold and pulled by two sparkling sugar horses, raced by.

"Dear me." Mister Minty put his paw over his chest. "We're in deep trouble now."

"Why? Who is that?" I tightened my hold on Ava.

"That would be the evil queen, and she's found your sister."

Chapter 4

Before I could ask what he'd meant, the horses and carriage turned around and raced toward us. The horses stopped abruptly and reared up on their hind legs, neighing. Sparkling sugar fluttered from their manes and glittered on the roadway.

A young woman, maybe around twenty-years-old, stepped from the carriage. She wore a long ice-blue dress with white fur trim around her throat and wrists. An icicle crown sat on top of her long, straight platinum-blonde hair and her eyes looked like the blue of a glacier.

"Mister Minty, just where do you think you're taking my daughter?" The woman's loud voice thundered, and the rabbit began quivering.

He scampered behind me as the queen moved closer toward us. Ava broke free from my grip and stood at my side.

"You can't pretend I don't know you've been planning on kidnapping my daughter."

"No, Queen Frosting, your Majesty, I was bringing her to your palace."

"Quiet! I'll turn you into a chocolate bunny if you oppose me." She glided toward us and stopped directly in front of Ava. She knelt down and gave my sister a hug and a kiss on her forehead. "Welcome home, daughter. I have waited many long years for your return to me."

The air surrounding us turned so cold it was hard to breathe. I expected Ava to pull away from the evil queen and the cold, but instead, she shocked me by returning the hug.

"What are you talking about? Ava's my little sister. My mother is her mother, and you aren't our family." My breath caught in my throat as the words tumbled out of my mouth.

"Quiet, human. Do not dare to compare yourself to Queen Frosting's princess." She pulled my sister toward the gold-trimmed carriage. "Come, darling. I have prepared a banquet to welcome you home and celebrate your release from banishment."

"Wait! You can't take her." I tugged on Ava's arm. "She's my family. I have to make sure she gets home safely to our parents."

I tried to pull Ava back. The queen lifted a sparkling icy scepter and pointed it at me. Snowball cupcakes shot out and knocked me down. Some of the coconut icing flew into my mouth, which I still had wide open from shock. The creamy sweet icing was good. Really good, probably the best I've ever tasted. But I still wasn't going to let that woman steal my baby sister.

"Cool." Ava practically jumped up and down and a huge grin lit up her face. It was the first word she'd said since Queen Frosting had shown up. "How'd you do that?"

"Magic, of course." The queen bent down and placed Ava's rosy cheeks between her palms. "Soon you will be able to do that and much more."

"Really? Can I try now?"

"Certainly, my child." She handed Ava the scepter. "Just concentrate and your mind will tell the magic what to do."

Ava pointed the scepter at Mister Minty and grinned.

I groaned. No good thing could come from a sugar-wired kid getting ahold of magic. And, I was right.

Jelly beans flew out of his long, green ears. As he hopped around, the jelly beans became flying missiles while his squeals filled the air. A few jelly beans pelted my arms and one came close to hitting my cheek.

"Ouch!" I glared at the queen. She should have known this wasn't a good idea, but instead, she stood there with a proud smile on her cold face. "Knock it off, Ava. That's not a nice thing to do."

"I'll stop if he tells me that he's the Easter Bunny."

Despite the jelly beans streaming from both of his ears, Mister Minty stood straight and tried to look as dignified as possible. "I will do no such thing, Your Highness. I am a royal ambassador for King Cookie himself."

The Queen took her scepter back and the jelly bean

flight slowed to a trickle, then finally stopped. "Excellent, my child. Your magic is even stronger than I thought."

"That was fun. Can I do it again? Please?" Ava jiggled up and down on her toes and clapped her hands.

"Certainly. We will start your training tomorrow." The queen lifted Ava up and placed her into the carriage.

I ran toward them, wanting to tell Ava to come back, that I loved her, and she needed to stay with me. Before I could get even a single word out of my mouth, the Queen picked up a long black licorice whip and cracked it over the horses' heads. The carriage lurched and then raced down the road.

Chapter 5

"Ava, wait! Come back! Please?" My throat felt sore, and my words sounded hoarse after yelling. I had hoped my sister would hear me and turn back. I couldn't lose her. Mom and Dad would ground me for the rest of my life, and strangely, I was ready to admit that I would miss that little shrimp if she weren't around. I stared at the now empty road.

I felt a tug on my T-shirt. The green rabbit looked like he was about to burst into tears.

"I'm sorry, Princess."

"Really, I'm not a princess. Please just call me Amber."

"Your Highness, I cannot. It would be inappropriate for me to be disrespectful." His ears and whiskers drooped even lower. "I tried getting you and your sister on your way to Bonbon Castle before she found you. I have failed you and the citizens of our land."

I felt sorry for him, so I reached out and gave the Ambassador a quick pat on his shoulder. The smell of peppermint filled the air. "Don't worry Mister Minty. I'm sure we can figure out how to get Ava back. Can't we?"

"Perhaps we should make our way to the castle and ask the Duke of Custard. If anyone knows what to do, it will be him."

The green rabbit, looking paler than when I had met him just a short time ago, began hopping down the sugar rock road. Despite being the same height as me, his leaps covered at least ten feet with each bound. I stood there and watched him move further away. How would I ever keep up?

He stopped in the middle of the road and looked back at me. "Your Highness, we must hurry. I worry Queen Frosting may change her mind and return for you."

"And that's a bad thing?"

"Of course, Your Highness. The queen is evil. Evil, I tell you."

"What does she want with my sister? She's not going to hurt her, is she?"

"Have no fear. The Queen will take excellent care of Princess Ava. That is, if you call corrupting your sister, excellent care." His ears twitched almost uncontrollably. "At any rate, she will not harm her."

He bounded further away, and I hurried to catch up. Not an easy thing to do wearing dollar store flip-flops. "Can you please explain what's going on? I've got to be in the middle of the weirdest dream ever."

I looked down at my jean shorts and Taylor Swift T-shirt. The same shirt that I'd spilled soda on two weeks ago and Mom couldn't get the stain out. Usually, when you're in a dream, you either have pajamas on or almost nothing at all. My shorts and T-shirt were what I'd been wearing all day before this crazy dream started. It was my sister who'd been wearing PJs, but this was my dream, not hers.

"This is a dream, right?"

"No, Your Highness. This is real." He bounded again and I wondered if he had springs on his bottom paws. "Now please keep up. We have a long way to travel before it gets dark."

"Why don't you have a car or horses like the queen?"

"Car? What's a car?" Mister Minty paused and looked back at me. His paws twitched as if he wanted to wave me forward at a faster speed.

"A vehicle, kind of like the queen's carriage, except it runs with a mechanical or electrical motor."

"Hum, maybe the Duke knows about your odd contraption."

"If you don't have cars, why don't you use horses like the queen?"

His ears quivered then drooped down to his shoulders. I heard him sigh. "Your Highness, those poor creatures were once citizens of Sweet Treats Kingdom."

"You mean the horses used to be on your side and now they're working for the queen?"

"Not exactly." His nose twitched and his eyes filled up

with green liquid. "They were people and animals who displeased Queen Frosting. She placed an evil curse on them and now they toil for her. Horses were only mythical monsters in a storybook until she brought her curse."

I gasped, finally realizing our situation was even worse than I thought. Not only were we lost and had no idea how to find our way home, my baby sister had been kidnapped by a demented witch. She didn't deserve the title of queen.

I broke into a trot, trying to catch back up to the rabbit. "Can't someone fight the queen and free your citizens?"

"Our legend foretells of a golden child who will break the spell and free our kingdom. We've been waiting for your sister to arrive."

"I'm telling you, it can't be Ava. She's only five. Besides, she has a bad temper and you've seen what sugar does to her."

"It has to be your sister. Our kingdom is on the verge of being completely taken over by the evil queen." He sat on a tree stump, which looked like it was made of chocolate, and huffed. "Princess Ava has unusually strong magic for a child her age. She's supposed to rescue us but, now that the queen has the princess and her powers, I fear all is lost."

"Perhaps the Duke will know what to do?"

"He sent me to this side of the kingdom, as a lookout, to find your sister when she arrived. He's counting on the golden child just as much as I am." He peered up at me. "Are you magical like your sister? Maybe you can help."

"Who me? Nope. I'm not magical at all." My voice

squeaked. Not only was I not magical, I wasn't brave either. I only wanted to go home and forget this entire nightmare. But I realized that wouldn't happen until someone figured out how to rescue my little sister.

Chapter 6

Mister Minty led the way down the rock candy road for a while, before turning off onto a dirt path. I bent down and looked closely, then picked up a few crumbs. The path was made of crushed chocolate cookies. Mister Minty had slowed his hopping and bounding, once he realized I couldn't keep up, but he didn't like my delay. "Princess, we can't risk stopping even for a moment."

While I wanted to rush to find someone who could rescue my sister, I couldn't help but pause, every now and then, to examine the candy and sweets used for common things. Like the roads. I straightened up and brushed the crumbs from my hands. "Sorry. I'll try to keep up."

The path led through forests of pine trees that looked like upside-down ice cream cones covered with dark green icing piped on. It smelled just like the waffle cones my mom bought for me the last time she took me to the Orange County Fair. And, for the record, I didn't get cotton candy and an Icee to eat with my ice cream either. I'm not a sugar fiend like my sister plus, my Mom has more common sense than my Dad.

By the time we walked into the forest, the sun had started sinking behind the trees. Dusk crept upon us making it harder to see what lay ahead on the path. Mister Minty kept looking over his shoulder as if to see what lurked in the deep shadows of the trees. He made me nervous.

"How much further do we have to walk?" I tried not to complain, but my flip-flops weren't made for trekking long distances.

"I hope we'll make it to the house in less than a half-hour." He looked back at me then increased his long bounding hops. "Can you walk faster, your Highness?"

I was limping by then, thanks to blisters that had formed between my toes. "I'll try. Aren't we going to the castle?"

"I didn't realize how slow you traveled. We won't make it before nightfall. I think we'd better spend the night at the Toffee House." He peered back into the trees. "Strange creatures have been reported recently, coming out once the sun sets. I can't risk your safety."

I shivered. What did he mean by strange creatures? So far, I'd seen nothing but strange creatures since arriving here.

"Can we eat the toffee?" My stomach growled. "Do they have something else besides candy to eat?"

The rabbit nodded his head, his ears flopping up and

down. "They will have cakes and cookies."

"No, I mean something besides sweets and sugar."

"Whatever do you mean, Princess?" He stopped and looked back at me.

"At home, we eat pizza, hamburgers, hotdogs, chips . . . and mom makes us eat vegetables. You know, stuff like that."

"I'm sorry, I'm not familiar with that type of food. I'm sure the Gingerbread Clan will find something that will appeal to you."

"Ooh, gingerbread people? With vanilla icing? Can I eat one of those?" It was my favorite cookie in the whole wide world and one of the reasons Christmas was my favorite holiday.

Mister Minty turned and looked at me. His nostrils flared and his mouth hung wide open. His fur looked a bit yellowish in the dim light.

"If Your Highness commands it, they will provide one of the younger children for your meal." He shivered from the top of his ears to the bottom of his paws before turning a deeper shade of yellow.

"Ewww! I am totally not talking about eating a real, live gingerbread man!" I felt like I had started to turn shades of yellow as well once I realized what Mister Minty thought. "At home, we have cookies decorated with candy and icing. Are you telling me you have people made out of gingerbread?"

"Of course, Princess." He shook his head. "I can't begin to imagine the world you come from. It worries me what the queen will do with that knowledge once your sister tells her."

With that, the rabbit bounded off down an even narrower path, the trees closing in on us. I shivered, wondering what could be hiding behind those sugar cones when I heard a rustling sound, then a crunch. I broke into a trot and hurried to catch him. In my haste, another blister broke out on my foot, forcing me to slow down as I limped with each step. I was ready to ditch the flip-flops but, just when I thought I couldn't take another step, a golden glow cut through the growing darkness. I stumbled, almost knocking over Mister Minty, who'd stopped in a clearing that contained several small houses.

Bright yellow light spilled from windows cut into slabs of toffee. The candy had been molded into the shape of small houses. When we got closer, I saw there were about ten homes lining the clearing. Towering trees abutted the backs of the houses. Small marshmallow Peep birds flitted from the branches and a few bravely swooped down to a rooftop and pecked at the nuts embedded into the roof.

Smoke rose lazily from the chimney of the house closest to us. It filled the air with the smell of buttery, sweet sugar and my tummy rumbled.

"Hello? Sir William?" Mister Minty's voice took on a strong British accent as he hollered.

The door, from the house closest to where we stood, was thrown open. A chubby ginger man stepped through the doorway and ambled toward us. His hair was a reddish color, and his cheeks were bright pink. His eyes sparkled like green glass marbles and matched the color of his suspenders, bow tie, and trousers. The white shirt he wore was trimmed with red rick rack. I'd learned about rick rack at a sewing camp my mom sent me to last summer. It's really a zig-zag trim and even my teacher had no idea where the name came from. Several small boys, looking just like Sir William, were dressed identically to him. They followed close behind the gingerbread man.

"Mister Minty, welcome!" Sir William's voice was deep with a slow drawl that made me think of honey. "What brings you to our Gingerbread Settlement?"

"I'm hoping we can find shelter with you tonight." He pointed back to me. "It seems the prophecy is becoming a reality. Not one, but two royal princesses were dropped from the clouds today."

The young ginger boys whooped and danced behind their father.

Mister Minty's whiskers drooped, and his voice fell into a hoarse whisper. "Unfortunately, the evil queen managed to capture the Golden One. She's taken our princess to Cinnamon Castle."

Chapter 7

"I managed to save the Golden One's sister, though." Mister Minty, the royal Ambassador, stood straighter and puffed out his chest. "May I present Her Highness, Princess Amber."

Even though the Ambassador had done his best to put a positive spin on the situation, I could hear the disappointment in his voice. He'd rather have saved Ava. I was expendable, the non-golden one.

"Hello." I knelt down when the young boys peeked out from between the legs of their father. They had hidden there at the mention of the evil queen. "Mister Minty is taking me to see the Duke of Custard. He's going to figure out how to get my sister, um I mean, Princess Ava back."

Small lanterns that hung from the trees above me flickered on and caught my attention. I could see small round tan objects hanging from the branches. I wondered if that was what they made the toffee from.

The boys crept closer to me and the bravest reached out to touch my arm. I jumped when I felt the roughness of his hand. He scampered out of reach. A braver brother reached out and touched my curly black hair.

"It's so soft." He looked back at his brothers as he touched his own hair.

Up close, I could finally see that the boys were not flesh and blood like me. Instead, they were gingerbread. Their features were made from icing and candy, and the smell of cinnamon and sugar hung in the air whenever they moved or spoke. The boys' hair was stiff and spiky and had the same reddish hue as their father's hair.

"Don't be afraid. I won't hurt you." I reached out my hand. The boys must've decided I wouldn't eat them because they crept closer. I wondered if they knew about my conversation with Mister Minty. Soon, all seven of the young boys encircled me, their rough hands patting my hair, my clothes, and my skin.

"What are you made of?" a squeaky voice asked.

Their father's deep laugh echoed in the dim light. "Forgive their curiosity. They haven't been allowed to leave the forest since the queen began casting her curses. But where are my manners? Let me introduce my family. I am Sir William."

I've seen enough princess movies to know I was supposed to do something, so I stood up and curtsied. Sir William bowed back to me.

"My boys, Tripp and Tiger."

The one called Tiger roared and the other boys laughed.

"You can see where he got his nickname." Sir William chuckled. "My nephews, Trinity, Triton, Tristan, Trenton, and Tiga. And last but not least, my daughter, Trina."

Sir William looked around at the small faces surrounding him then turned back to the house and raised his voice. "Trina, come out here and greet our guests."

He turned back to me. "I apologize Princess Amber, she seems to be going through a shy phase."

A ginger girl slowly walked into the clearing. Her spiky hair was yellow and much longer than her brothers and cousins. She wouldn't look me in the eyes, but instead, offered a tiny curtsy.

"I'm pleased to meet you, Trina." I gave her a small bob of my own. "Thank you for providing shelter for us."

Instead of answering, she scowled then turned and went back to the house.

"Boys, go on inside and set the table for our guests. Make sure Trina has enough food set out for us. Mister Minty and I will be in soon."

"Yes, sir," they said in unison before they scampered back into the brightly lit house.

"They're good children, Sir William." Mister Minty watched them until the ginger boys were out of sight. "Considering what happened to their mothers and all."

My ears perked up. "What happened?"

Sir William exchanged a look with Mister Minty. The

same look that grown-ups give each other when they really don't want to tell you what's going on.

Mister Minty sighed. "Princess Amber needs to know, even if she's a child. After all, the queen has captured her sister and may be coming back for her."

Sir William nodded, then plopped himself onto the ground. It appeared his legs just gave out on him. "My wife and her two sisters were harvesting the Toffee Chips deep in the forest. A monster, a huge white giant puffy thing, charged them and swallowed each and every one of the women up."

A tear rolled down his cheek, leaving a dark track, and Mister Minty reached over and clasped his shoulder. I squatted down and patted his leg.

"Several of the Peeps flew to our cottage to tell us of the tragic news. My two brothers-in-law went to search for our wives, but they too disappeared. We can safely assume that the evil queen is behind this atrocity."

"How long ago did this happen?" I asked.

"Six months. Six long months. I'm raising the children on my own. The boys are doing okay, but it's Trina I worry about. She won't talk about it and becomes more and more withdrawn every day. A girl needs her mother, you know?"

"Unfortunately, this is just one of the many outrages that have happened lately." Mister Minty's head bobbed up and down. "I suppose you need to know what you're up against, Princess Amber."

Chapter 8

I gulped. "You mean there's more than this and the horses?"

"I'm afraid so." Mister Minty stroked his whiskers as if deep in thought. "We try to keep the bad news quiet so that folk won't panic, but it's a losing battle. Gossip spreads quicker than you can say S'more Shores."

"I heard something about Holly Clause missing." Sir William looked up at Mister Minty. "Is it true?"

"Unfortunately, yes. She was last seen picking candy canes along S'more Shores two days ago. All we could find were her shoes floating in the river. We tracked a strange set of large round prints from where Holly was last seen, but they disappeared into the forest."

"S'more Shores?" I liked the sound of that, although I should have been more concerned about this Holly person. I fleetingly wondered if she was related to Santa but when my stomach rumbled, my attention was diverted.

"Yes. Where the chocolate river meets the graham cracker sand."

"I guess all you need are some marshmallows for dipping." I smacked my lips together. My dad's work Christmas party always had chocolate fondue. The chocolate flowed out of a three-tiered fountain, and it was my favorite thing at the party. Chocolate-covered marshmallows sprinkled with graham cracker crumbs made it one of the best desserts ever . . . next to mint chocolate chip ice cream, of course.

Sir William looked at me and his eyes almost bugged out of his sockets. His mouth pinched tight and turned down at the corners.

"Don't worry, Sir William." Mister Minty placed a hand on the ginger man's trembling shoulder. "Princess Amber's homeland is not like our realm. Their marshmallows are not, I presume, living creatures."

"Your marshmallows are alive?" Uh-oh, I forgot, again, that food at home wasn't food here. But I had to ask even though I already knew the answer.

"Yes, Your Highness. Marshmallow Peeps are our birds."

"Father? Trina says dinner is waiting." A small voice floated over the clearing.

"Alright, son. We'll be right in." Sir William looked at us and rubbed his face. Small bits of cookie rubbed off and flitted to the ground. "Any other bad news Mister Minty?"

"Just rumors of strange beasts around the Maple Syrup Swamp, but nothing definite." The green rabbit pointed to the house. "Shall we have dinner?"

I'd made it halfway thru the door when a blue rabbit hopped into the clearing. His breath was labored, and he wheezed so heavily I thought he might fall over. He bent over at the waist and rested his paws on his legs. With every breath he blew out, I could smell blueberries filling the air.

"Mister Minty." He noisily sucked in air. "Mister Minty, you must hasten to the Duke's villa right away!"

"What's this, Mister Periwinkle? What's happened now?"

"The Duke of Custard seems to have broken his leg. He told me to send you rapidamente." Mister Periwinkle remained bent over at the waist, his breathing still noisy. "I've been hopping all over the kingdom looking for you since this morning. I haven't even stopped for a bite to eat."

My ears perked up. Rapidamente was Italian for quickly. Was the Duke Italian? Like my real father?

"How did the Duke manage to do that?" Mister Minty shook his head. "Don't tell me he's been skiing again."

"Yes, but it wasn't the skiing that broke his leg. He was trying to get away from some huge puffy monster that started chasing him down the slopes." Mister Periwinkle pulled on Mister Minty's paw. "Please, we have to leave right away. The Duke fears an invasion from the evil queen's forces is imminent."

Mister Minty looked from Sir William to my feet. "I don't know what to do with Princess Amber. I don't think she'll be able to finish the journey tonight."

I looked at my feet and saw blood where the blisters had popped between my toes.

"Perhaps Sir William can deliver her to the castle tomorrow." Mister Periwinkle pointed at the ginger man. "No matter what, it is imperative that you reach the Duke tonight."

A frown creased Sir William's forehead. "I couldn't possibly leave the children by themselves, especially after what's happened to their mothers. Maybe she can stay here until you can come back for her?"

Mister Minty shook his head. "If the queen is gathering her forces, we can't risk the princess being out here any longer than necessary. Mister Periwinkle, can you stay and escort her to the castle tomorrow?"

"Impossible. I am in charge of warning our citizens and must be on my way immediately." With that, the blue rabbit bowed low to us and then bounded back out into the darkness.

"Father?" A sweet voice sounded next to us. "I can take Princess Amber to the castle."

Trina tugged at her father's arm. "I know the way since Mother's taken me to sell the Toffee Chips for the last ten years. I've been going since I was five."

"I can't risk your safety, my dear." He clasped his daughter's hands tightly. "I couldn't bear it."

"I'm not any safer here than going to the castle." Trina scowled. "If the queen is invading, none of us are safe no matter where we are. Princess Amber must reach the castle and help the Duke defeat her."

My mouth dropped open. This wasn't the Trina I had met minutes ago, who wouldn't talk or barely acknowledged me.

"I'm afraid that's the only solution we have Sir William. I'm not happy about having to rely on children to protect our realm, but I suppose we must use what we have." Mister Minty cleared his throat. "Trina, please take Princess Amber to the castle as quickly as you can. You must leave by daybreak. Your father will tell you which areas to avoid and the safest roads to follow."

With those words, Mister Minty bowed to me and then bounded down the same path Mister Periwinkle had taken moments before.

Chapter 9

"Come along children. Trina and Princess Amber need to eat and have time to rest. They have a long journey ahead of them."

I sat, squeezed in between Trina and Sir William, on one of the long benches that lined a huge wooden table. Platters of peanut brittle, carrot cake, candy corn, and maple syrup cookies sat in the middle. As soon as Sir William filled my plate with some of each, the boys grabbed handfuls of candy corn and began stuffing their mouths.

Sir William rolled his eyes and shook his head. "Since their mothers disappeared, I can't get them to use any manners. Please forgive us, Princess."

"It's okay. I'm sure this is how my sister would eat candy if she were here." I smiled at the boys even though I wanted to cry. I missed that little shrimp.

In between mouthfuls of sticky candy, the ginger boys asked me about my world and my family. With each fact I shared, they exclaimed over and over how strange earth was. Trina reverted back to her silent self, scowling at me when I dared ask her a question. I tried to ignore her as best as I could, which wasn't easy since we were squished around the table. Every time I picked up a piece of candy, my arm would brush against her rough one. I wondered if she regretted volunteering to guide me on such a dangerous trip, leaving her family behind.

Sir William's voice cut into my thoughts. "Trina, bring your extra shoes and let the princess try them on. It's obvious if you're going to reach the castle tomorrow, she needs something more comfortable for her feet."

He had me sit in a rocking chair then knelt in front of me and carefully cleaned and bandaged each foot. Trina appeared at his shoulder and handed him the shoes. They were brown and looked soft, kind of like moccasins. I could tell, by looking at them, that they were going to be too small.

Sir William held them against my feet and shook his head. "Trina, bring my shoes."

When she returned, he slipped them gently onto my feet, taking care not to bump my bandaged blisters. They were a perfect fit with a bit of extra room at the tip so I could wiggle my toes.

"Ah, that feels so much better." I stood and took a few steps to try them out.

One of the boys kicked his shoes off and slipped his feet

into my flip-flops.

"How do you walk in these things?" His feet flapped against the polished toffee floor and he swung his arms trying to regain balance. "I can't believe you wear things that hurt."

"Tripp, please give the shoes back to the princess." Sir William's voice was firm. "I'm sorry Your Highness, the boys have once again been neglecting their manners."

"It's okay, I know they're curious just like my sister would be." My eyes began to sting as I thought about Ava. I worried about her being scared all on her own and worried that I might never see her again.

Sir William showed me to Trina's room and gave me a nightshirt. I assumed it was his wife's nightie, since Trina was at least ten inches shorter than I was. "Good night Princess. I will wake you in time to leave with the rising sun. I hope you sleep well."

Once he closed the door, I looked around Trina's bedroom. A small bed featuring a fluffy pink comforter was placed in the corner. Her walls were polished toffee and it looked like she used them to practice her icing decorating skills. Vanilla icing piped into colorful flowers, animals, and landscaping decorated the walls. Some designs were random while others looked like they told a story. On the furthest wall from the bed, she had created a map of the kingdom. The Gingerbread Clan was prominently situated in the middle. I wondered how accurate the map was because it looked like we still had a very long walk to get to the castle.

Once I blew out the lantern, I tossed and turned on

Trina's soft bed. Even though I was exhausted by the forced march with Mister Minty, I didn't fall asleep until the moon had traveled halfway across the sky. I couldn't stop worrying about my baby sister. Morning came much too soon, and when Trina knocked on the bedroom door, I saw the sky had just started to turn rosy pink.

"Breakfast is ready," she whispered into my dark room.

"Okay, I'll be right there." I jumped out of bed and groaned. My feet ached and the blisters between my toes made me wish I could stay in bed. But instead, I dressed and put Sir William's shoes on before I joined the family at the kitchen table.

The ginger boys were quiet as they sat around the table. Trina only stared at the honey cake sitting on her plate while Sir William acted like my dad did after drinking too much coffee. He'd sit down then jump up and grab something from the cupboard, then rush to the sink, then plop back down at the table before repeating the process all over again.

"Dad," Trina spoke in a hushed voice, "it's going to be okay. I'll get the princess to the castle, and I'll be back home before you know it."

"I've been giving it some thought, and I think you should stay in Candy Village for a while. You'll be safer that way." Sir William pulled a red pouch from his front pocket. "Here are some coins. Get a room at the Cupcake Inn and I can rest assured you'll be safe staying there."

"Trina can stay with me." I volunteered but then realized I had no idea where I would be staying myself nor did I have any coins. "Er, I'm sure the Duke or Mister Minty will find us both a place."

"Humph, I suppose it's time you girls were on your way." Sir William pulled his daughter into a tight hug and then handed her the red pouch and a well-worn backpack. "Stay away from S'more Shores. You'll have to cut through Maple Syrup Swamp instead and climb Popsicle Peak. But be extra careful, the swamp seems to be spreading and it's stickier than ever."

"Yes, Father."

"Thank you, Sir William, for your hospitality. I'm sure the Duke will thank you for your kindness as well."

We made our way to the clearing, while the young ginger boys trailed behind us. They stopped before they reached the trail leading through the trees. The sun had already peeked over the candy cone trees and then it disappeared as we walked deeper into the forest. Dark gloom surrounded us.

Chapter 10

Even though Trina was quite a bit shorter than me, she walked fast. It was all I could do to keep up.

"How long will it take for us to reach the castle?" I hoped it would be less than an hour. My feet were still tired and sore. It would take a few days, with my feet propped up, for my blisters to heal.

Trina turned and glared at me. "If you'd walk faster, we can make it by lunchtime."

"It's that far?" This wasn't the news I'd wanted. "I'm going as fast as I can. My blisters still hurt."

Trina rolled her green eyes at me, flipped her spiky hair over her shoulder, and walked even faster. I wondered where the nice ginger girl, who had volunteered to lead me last night, had gone. Maybe she wasn't a morning person. I know I'm not, but I try not to be rude to other people. Well . . .

maybe to my little sister, but certainly not to friends or people I had just met.

I jogged a bit to catch up but knew I couldn't keep the pace without collapsing soon. "I want to say thank you for volunteering to take me. It can't be easy leaving your family behind with everything that's happened."

Trina just grunted then put extra space between us. I jogged some more until I reached her side. "Look, if you're mad at me or something, can you tell me? I'm sorry you had to leave your family."

She stopped and whirled to face me so quickly that I almost knocked her over. Her face was scrunched, and her lips trembled. "It's your fault, Princess. If you and your sister hadn't decided you needed to come save the kingdom, the evil queen would have left us alone. My mom would still be alive."

Trina said "princess" like it was a dirty word. She was mad, really mad, but it wasn't my fault.

"First of all, I am not a princess, so you can call me Amber. Just plain Amber. Secondly, my sister and I hadn't even heard of your kingdom until we fell onto the blue Jell-O trampoline yesterday." Technically that wasn't exactly true. Ava and I had been playing the Sweet Treats board game but I never, ever would have believed it was a real place. "I have no idea how we got here or why, but that evil queen kidnapped my sister and I have to find someone who can rescue her."

"Really? You're not a princess?" Trina didn't seem so mad. "Why do you let everyone think that?"

"Because you know grownups, they never listen to what a kid has to say."

That made Trina smile. I guess kids are treated the same no matter what land they live in.

"I'm sorry I was mean to you. I've listened to stories for the last year about how the Golden One would save us from the evil queen and I was mad that you didn't show up in time to save my mom and aunts."

"I'm sorry my sister and I can't help you. I think there's been a terrible mistake and I just want to find Ava and go home."

Trina nodded then turned around and started walking down the narrow path. She set a slower pace this time, but I noticed her shoulders were sagging and her head was bent forward. I thought I heard a sniffle, but then again, maybe it was a bird hiding in one of the trees.

We walked for about an hour, neither one of us saying a word. The forest was very quiet, not at all like the woods where my family goes camping every August. Here, there were no birds chirping, or bugs buzzing. Squirrels weren't chattering, nor were lizards scrambling for cover. Trina held up her hand as she came to a sudden stop and then put her index finger to her red lips.

Just beyond Trina, was the edge of the forest and a meadow spread out beyond the trees.

Trina placed her mouth close to my ear and whispered. "Let's rest here for a bit and make sure nothing is hiding or waiting for us out there."

I shivered at the thought then followed Trina's example and plopped myself onto the ground, hidden behind a large bush. I smelled mint and looked closer at the leaves. They were spearmint gummy leaves. Trina picked one off and popped it into her mouth before offering me one along with a honey cake from her backpack.

We silently waited and ate our snacks for about fifteen minutes before Trina stood up and waved me forward. "I haven't seen any movement out there nor have I heard anything. It should be safe to go now."

I followed her into the bright sunlight and blinked my eyes. I hadn't realized how dark and closed in the forest had been beneath the thick trees.

Trina pointed at a mountain about two miles away. Something white shimmered at the top. "That's the beginning of the Duke's land. Once we cross Popsicle Peak, we should be safe."

"That's the mountain we have to climb?" My voice squeaked and I shuddered wondering how I was going to climb something so tall when my feet were already so tired.

"It's not as bad as it looks. The trails are easy to follow and it's mostly safe."

"Uh, what do you mean mostly safe?" That sounded like somewhere I didn't want to be.

"It gets narrow at the peak, but it's fine as long as the wind isn't blowing."

I started to ask her about the white monster that had tried to attack the Duke the day before, then remembered Trina hadn't been there when Mister Periwinkle had shared the news. I decided it could wait until we reached the mountain. There wasn't any sense in causing her to worry about anything else for now.

Trina chose a narrow stone path choked with brambles, cattails, and trailing licorice whips. We had to step carefully so that we didn't get poked with the bramble thorns or tripped by the licorice. As slow and careful as we walked, a whip still managed to wrap itself around Trina's leg. She fell, face first. I heard a crunch and ran to help her up.

"Are you alright, Trina?" I pulled her by the waist to help her stand. "Did you get hurt?"

Trina looked down then back at me. Tears collected in her eyes, but she shook her head. "I'm a klutz. Come on, we need to keep moving."

When she started walking again, she cradled her arm in front of her body. I took a step to follow and heard a crunch beneath my foot. When I lifted my shoe, I saw I had just crushed Trina's gingerbread hand.

Chapter 11

"Trina, you're hurt!" I felt shaky and my knees wanted to collapse. How could I tell her I had just demolished her hand? "Is there a doctor around here who can help you?"

She shook her head. "It'll have to wait until we get to the castle. Come on Amber, we need to hurry."

"But, but you lost your hand, and ewwww, I just stepped on it!" I felt queasy. "I think I destroyed it. I am so, so sorry!"

"It'll be okay. Right now, we have to get out of here or something worse might happen."

I couldn't believe how calm Trina acted, but even though I wanted to throw up, I stepped behind her. As I followed the ginger girl on the tangled path, I wondered what could be worse than losing your hand. The path we walked on meandered around the edge of the meadow instead of going through it. If we were in a hurry to get out of this place, it seemed like we were wasting time following the zigzagging trail.

"Wouldn't it be faster if we walked straight across the meadow instead of going around?"

"I forgot. You don't know our land, do you? Whatever you do, stay on this path and don't wander off. This is Maple Syrup Swamp. One step in the wrong direction and its stickiness will drag you under."

"This is the swamp? It looks more like the meadow Bambi was in when his mother was killed."

"Who is Bambi and why was his mother killed? Do you have an evil queen too?" Trina turned sideways to hear my answer.

Unfortunately, she didn't stop walking and, instead, stepped off the path and into the swamp. Immediately, a sucking sound happened, and her leg sank up to her knee which made her lose her balance. Before I could grab her, her second leg was in the gooey mess.

"Quick, grab hold of my hand." I planted my feet onto the stone path and leaned over the tangle of weeds hiding the lethal swamp.

Trina allowed me to grab her remaining hand and pull but then screamed when we both heard a snap. Her cookie arm had a crack at her elbow, and I knew if I pulled any harder, her entire arm would detach. I swallowed down my panic even though the syrup was up to Trina's thighs now. She was sinking fast.

I yanked several long licorice whips off their roots and

threw an end to Trina. "Here, wrap this around your waist."

She struggled for a minute but then dropped the licorice. "I can't do it with only one hand. Just leave me here and save yourself. You need to reach the Duke so he can rescue your sister."

"I'm not leaving you." I tied a whip together lasso style. "Hang on, I'm going to try to loop this around you and pull you out."

After I'd tossed the whip at least a hundred times without catching Trina, my arms felt like lead. I shuddered when I saw the swamp had inched up to her waist. She'd kept her eyes closed most of the time as I'd tossed the makeshift lasso and continued to cradle her damaged arm.

"I'm going to get you out one way or another. Don't give up hope." I found some longer whips and braided them together, hoping they would be long enough to loop behind her.

I tried and tried and just when I thought I couldn't lift my arm for even a second more, the licorice braid landed on top of her head. Trina grabbed it with her remaining hand and pulled it down to her waist. I dug my feet in and started to pull her toward safety. The Maple Syrup Swamp didn't want to let her go and for every few inches I pulled her forward, the swamp pulled her right back in. My arms and back muscles burned from the effort, and I could see panic building on Trina's face.

"Can you move your legs to help me?"

"No, I'm stuck." Trina's voice quivered. "I'm afraid

they'll crack if I push hard."

Oh boy, I didn't see how I could get her out if she didn't help. "Alright. I'm going to try a different angle and see if that helps."

I moved about six steps down the path, and let the braided whip slip carefully through my fingers. The last thing we needed was for me to drop it into the swamp. If I did, there would be no hope for saving Trina.

I stopped and turned to face the ginger girl again. "I'm going to start pulling and when I say go, you need to kick with your legs. I know you don't want to risk cracking them, but if you don't help, I don't think I can pull you out by myself. Okay?"

She hesitated, nodded her head, then gripped the licorice whip tightly with her one hand.

"Okay, go!" I yelled at the top of my lungs, dug in my heels, and pulled with every muscle I had in my body. I was ready to whoop when I felt her move about twelve inches toward me, but then my foot slipped on a pebble. And then the other foot tangled with the long licorice lasso. And then I slid straight into the swamp.

Chapter 12

"Oomph." My breath was knocked from my lungs when I hit the sticky maple syrup. I immediately sank into the gooey mess, all the way up to my knees. The licorice whip lasso disappeared from sight, sucked into the brown goo lurking beneath the marshy grass.

"Amber!" Trina screeched. "I knew you should have left me and saved yourself. This is all my fault."

"Don't panic." I said it more for myself than for Trina because I really wanted to start crying. "I'll figure something out."

I struggled to pull a foot up and step forward but instead, I was sucked further down. The situation was even worse than I'd thought. "Um, has anyone ever tried getting out of this like you're supposed to be able to do in quicksand?"

"What's quicksand?"

"Never mind." I didn't see how laying down in this sticky stuff and rolling would help. Syrup is completely different than quicksand, not that I'd ever been in quicksand. I'd just read about it in school and then watched some videos on YouTube. But I figured it couldn't hurt to try since I wasn't going to get out by walking.

I squatted down and tried to lay back. Instead of floating, the maple syrup sucked my butt in and before I knew it, I was waist-deep in the sticky goo. Now that I was covered with the swamp ick, I could fully smell the sweet maple. There was a strange undertone of sulfur and then I realized that the black licorice vines had added their aroma to the swamp. I hoped the smell wouldn't cling to my hair forever. I hadn't given up hope that I'd figure out a way to get out of this mess.

"Amber?" Trina's voice trembled and I could barely hear her. I turned my head toward her and saw the goo was up to her chest. "I'm so sorry I was mean to you earlier."

"It's okay, Trina."

"No, I have to say it now because we're going to die here."

Die? I didn't want to die. My life couldn't end like this. And who would rescue my little sister if I didn't find help?

"Help! Help us, please!" I screamed at the top of my lungs. "Come on Trina, scream with me. Maybe someone is around who can rescue us. We can't give up."

"But, what if there's a monster or the evil queen? We don't want them to hear us." Trina practically whimpered.

"Does it matter? We're goners anyway if we don't get

help." I sucked in a deep breath and screamed again, relieved that Trina had joined in.

What I hadn't realized before screaming my head off, was every time I took a deep breath in to yell, the swamp pulled me further down. Any little movement made me sink faster and faster. I wished I could say I was brave. But I'm not and it didn't take long for panic to set in. I started hyperventilating.

"Why aren't . . . you yelling anymore?" Trina panted and had a hard time getting her words out.

My heart pounded so hard and so fast that it sounded like a drum in my head. I tried to gulp in air. "I, I can't breathe."

"Don't give up yet." Trina's quiet voice sounded desperate.

I heard her words, but they sounded far away. Black specks floated across my eyes while sweat trickled down my scalp. I shook my head as hard as I could to clear my eyes and turned to look at Trina. The swamp sat just below her mouth, yet she still tried to yell for help. I couldn't let her down no matter how panicked I felt.

I sucked in a huge breath ignoring the syrup inching over my shoulders. In my shrillest voice, I screamed again, and again. "Help, help us, please! We're in the swamp!"

Just before the brown gunk crept over Trina's mouth, loud hooves pounded on stone, as something made its way along the path. A huge, glittering white horse came into view and slid to a stop in front of us. A shower of pebbles flew into the goo. Pink flowers were braided into its mane and tail, and it carried a ginormous candy cane in its mouth.

Trina whimpered and closed her eyes. I shivered knowing that horses were people cursed by the evil queen. Was it sent here to make sure we drowned in the swamp? Was it going to beat us over the head with the candy cane? I think I started to whimper too.

The horse neighed and reared on its hind legs before it sent the hooked end of the candy cane flying our way. I screeched and ducked my head, which plunged my face into the sticky goo. I pulled my head up and gagged. The sweet cloying goo clogged my nose and mouth and I coughed and sputtered to rid myself of the taste. I inhaled air to scream even louder but immediately swallowed the noise when I felt Trina bump into my back.

"Amber, we're moving. She's pulling us to shore." Trina wrapped her arm around my middle.

I wiped brown stickiness from my eyes and saw that the horse had hooked us with the curved end of her cane and pulled us toward the edge of the swamp. As happy as I was to be leaving the syrup, I was still frightened. Was the horse pulling us out so that it could eat us or take us to the evil queen? Were we out of the frying pan and into the fire so to speak? That was a saying Dad always liked to use on me.

Finally, free of the sucky swamp, Trina and I collapsed on the stone pathway. Breathing hard and still gagging a bit on the maple goo that had filled my mouth, I waited to be attacked. Instead, the horse bowed in front of me.

"Welcome to our land, Golden One."

"Uh, thank you but I think you've got me confused with my sister." I pushed my sticky hair out of my eyes. "And thank you for rescuing us. We were almost goners."

Trina chimed in, her voice shaky as she tried not to cry. "Yes, thank you. I didn't think we'd ever get out of there alive."

The horse turned her blue eyes toward me. "You are mistaken, Princess Amber. You are the Golden One."

"No, everyone knows it's Ava. You know . . . the golden hair and all that." I lifted my black matted hair which had started to get crunchy as the sugary syrup dried. "That's why the evil queen kidnapped her."

"How did you get us out of there?" Trina asked. "Amber and I couldn't even move our feet."

"I still have a bit of magic left in my cane that Queen Frosting overlooked." The horse attached the candy cane to her woven mane. "It comes in handy once in a while."

"Who are you? Er, I mean who were you before the curse?" I was afraid I would insult the horse after she'd rescued us.

The horse neighed and I hoped it meant she was laughing. "I'm Princess Sugarpop, no matter what shape or form I may be in."

Trina immediately curtsied and pulled my shirt in an attempt to have me do the same. I could take a hint, so I curtsied alongside her.

Princess Sugarpop nudged us up with her nose. "No time for formalities girls. We need to get you on your way so that the Golden One can fulfill her destiny."

I did not like the sound of that. It was bad enough that people thought Ava was the Golden One, but it was much worse if they thought it was me. I didn't have any idea how to rescue or save anyone, much less an entire kingdom. I was just a girl, had no magical powers, and was a scaredy-cat on top of that.

"Why are you calling me that, Princess Sugarpop? I don't have gold hair and I'm certainly not magical like my sister."

"Princess Amber, what color eyes do you have?"

"Amber, that's why my mom gave me that name."

"And what color is amber?"

And then I got it and my stomach flipped over. Amber was kind of a gold color, and I did have gold flecks in my eyes. Oh no. I did not want to be the Golden One!

Chapter 13

Trina looked at me then quickly sank into a curtsy. "Your Highness. I beg your forgiveness for not treating you with proper respect earlier."

"Get up, Trina. I'm just the same old Amber I always was." I glared at the horse. "I'm sure this is some kind of misunderstanding."

I wanted to make a snarky remark that they must be really desperate if they thought I could save them. But when I saw Trina's hopeful face, I bit my tongue. She'd already been through enough after suffering the loss of her mother and aunts.

"I would offer to give you girls a ride to the base of the Duke's mountain, but I'm afraid with all that maple syrup you'd stick to my back, and I'd never get you down." Princess Sugarpop started walking. "We need to hurry, so follow in my footsteps and you'll be fine."

With the sticky goo clinging to us, it wasn't long before our shoes were heavy blobs of pebbles and leaves. No matter how hard I tried, I couldn't scrape it off and each foot felt like it was ten pounds heavier than before our dunk in the swamp. I had a hard time keeping up with the horse and Trina prodded me in the back in an attempt to get me to walk faster.

"Princess Sugarpop?" Trina broke the silence. "Why did the evil queen turn you into a horse? Couldn't your magic protect you?"

"Queen Frosting, dear. You mustn't call her evil."

"But she is! She killed my mother and my aunts. Or I mean at least her monster did!"

"You must be mistaken, dear. My sister would never do anything like that."

I stopped mid-step and Trina crashed into me. "You mean the woman who kidnapped my sister is your sister? What happened? Why is she doing this? And what are you going to do to rescue my sister?"

The horse snorted and turned to face us. "Girls, we must hurry. I will tell you what I know if you walk faster."

Trina and I both agreed, but I wasn't sure I could go any faster with the growing blocks of debris on my feet.

"A year and a half ago Princess Frosting went to our father, King Cookie, and told him she was in love with the baker's son, Bob. They wanted to marry. He makes the most incredible caramel cinnamon rolls. Bob does, not my father.

I don't think my father knows how to bake anything."

"Anyway, King Cookie was furious and forbade her to ever see him again. To make sure she didn't disobey, he assigned two guards to keep an eye on her day and night. My sister was heartbroken." The horse quivered and swished her braided tail. "The king put together an expedition to search for a prince from neighboring kingdoms who would be worthy to marry his princess. My sister decided she would never marry anyone other than Baker Bob."

Princess Sugarpop was quiet for a few minutes. All that could be heard was heavy breathing and the clomping of my concrete block feet and the horse's hooves.

"Word came back a couple of months later that the expedition had found a prince, but the young man's parents wanted to meet my father before they allowed him to journey back to our kingdom. King Cookie left with a trusted ambassador. We have not heard from them since then."

"Haven't you sent search teams or whatever you call it here?" I asked.

"Anyone who leaves Sweet Treats Kingdom never returns." Princess Sugarpop sniffed then shuddered. "Not long after our father disappeared my sister declared herself queen. My father's advisors and ambassadors argued with her and then threatened to arrest her. That's when she left Bonbon Castle and started the curse."

"What about your mother? Couldn't she talk her out of cursing the kingdom?"

"Our mother died when I was born."

"Oh. I am so sorry." Me and my big mouth. I should have known there wasn't a mom around since Princess Sugarpop hadn't mentioned one. "Um, why did your sister turn you into a horse?"

"It's not as bad as you think. Frosting and I loved books about mythical creatures when we were younger, and horses were our favorite. When I was about eight years old, I said if I could choose what I wanted to be I would choose to be a horse."

"But she has to know you'd rather be a princess?" Horses were mythical creatures here? But walking and talking rabbits were normal?

"I think Frosting was afraid I would make myself queen and turn everyone against her. I was visiting her when she turned me into a horse. I haven't been home since I'm afraid people will fear me and try to destroy me." I could hear the hurt in her voice and thought I saw a tear drop from her brilliant blue eyes. "As long as I never visit home my sister gives me the freedom to come and go as I please. That's why I heard you yelling for help."

"I am so glad you did, Princess Sugarpop. Thank you again, for rescuing us." Trina sniffed and wiped her eyes. "But no matter what you say, she's an evil queen and she killed my mother."

Chapter 14

"I wish I could prove to you that she's not evil." Princess Sugarpop snorted. "But I'm not supposed to interfere with what she does."

"Or what? She'll turn you into something worse than a horse?" Trina sounded angry and she didn't seem afraid to yell at the princess. "Stop defending your sister and look at what she's doing to her family and to the kingdom!"

The horse shook her head. "She's all I have left. I'm not giving up on her."

"Excuse me." I waited until Trina and Sugarpop stopped glaring at each other, and I had their attention. "If I'm the Golden One and I'm supposed to defeat the evil queen, not that I'm saying she's evil, just repeating what I've been told, how am I supposed to do that? Am I supposed to kill her or arrest her or what?"

"No, no, no! You've got the prophecy wrong. You're supposed to break the evil curse. No one said anything about defeating or killing anyone. For all we know, my sister could be under an evil spell, making her do these things."

Princess Sugarpop really needed a reality check. Her sister was plain mean and had probably been a bully all her life. I'd had a couple of problems with bullies at school and I didn't want to deal with another one. "Okay, so I'm supposed to break the curse. Any ideas on how to do that?"

"You mean you don't know how?" Trina glared at me. "You're the Golden One. You're supposed to know what to do."

I shrugged. "Funny thing about that Golden One. I've never heard about it until yesterday."

Princess Sugarpop glared at me then shook her head. "Hurry up girls, time is growing short. You must cross the mountain before the afternoon winds start blowing." She broke into a trot without giving me another glance.

I think she was mad at me because she made us run for about twenty minutes with no breaks. I gasped for air and my legs felt shooting pains up and down them. Trina acted like it wasn't a problem, which made me cranky. The only good thing about the run was the pounding of my feet made the blocks of pebbles, dirt, and dried maple syrup fall off.

Finally, the horse abruptly stopped and turned toward us. "We're at the edge of the Duke's lands. I cannot go any further. Take this path over the mountain and once you cross Popsicle peak, you'll see the castle."

"Why can't you take us all the way?" I sounded whiny but I wasn't happy she'd made us run so fast for so long.

"I'm not allowed."

"But," I blurted out before the princess cut me off.

"Good bye, Golden One. Seek out the Duke and listen to his advice." With that, Princess Sugarpop kicked up her hind legs and then dashed back toward the swamp.

"What do we do now?" I stared at the tall peaks ahead of us.

"Climb the mountain and walk to the castle." Trina had a scowl on her face.

"Are you mad at me, too?" I knew I wasn't being very helpful, but this Golden One thing wasn't something I knew how to do. They had to have had it wrong. I could not be their rescuer.

"No, Your Highness." Trina's scowl remained. "Please follow me and try to keep up."

I looked up at the tallest peak and saw it was covered with white ice, while the lower slopes looked creamy. Being the Sweet Treats Kingdom, it was probably ice cream or something sweet. "Um, Trina? Is this the mountain that the Duke skis on?"

"Yes. The ski slopes are on the other side."

"I think I'd better mention something that Mister Minty told me."

"What now?" She turned toward me and gave me the look that my mom gives me when I'm procrastinating. I procrastinate often when it comes to homework and chores so I'm very familiar with that look.

"Just that a large white monster chased the Duke down the slopes when he was skiing two days ago. That's how he broke his leg. The Duke broke his leg, not the monster." I knew I was rambling but now that we were here, I didn't want to climb the mountain and see a monster. "Maybe this isn't such a good idea."

"You're just now telling me about this monster?" Trina had raised her voice and she sounded mad. "When it's too late to go a different way?"

"How was I supposed to know there was a different way? I'm not from around here you know!"

"Great, just great. We could have had an easy walk along S'more Shores and come in from the east. Nice flat graham cracker roads with no swamp to swallow us up or a mountain with monsters waiting to eat us." She rolled her eyes. "But no, you had to keep that information to yourself so now we have no choice."

"Didn't your dad tell us to avoid S'more Shores? That something bad happened to Holly Clause there?"

"It could've been rumors and besides no one actually saw anything happen. Unlike the Duke being chased by a monster." She shook her head and glared at me. "Come on. We have no choice now."

Chapter 15

Trina set a fast pace and it wasn't long before I, once again, wheezed and gasped for air. The lower part of the slope was barren. Dry rocky gray dirt for the most part with small olive-green shrubs trying to survive. Trina climbed rapidly, and I couldn't take the time to figure out what the dirt and shrubs were made of. Some kind of cookies or candy was my guess. As we reached higher elevations, large boulders littered the sides of the path, and shrubs had given up trying to live.

The air got colder the higher we climbed, and I shivered almost uncontrollably. I wished I had a jacket, but the cold didn't seem to affect Trina. If anything, she walked faster. When we reached the snow, I dipped my fingers in and picked up a scoop. Despite what I had told Ava about not putting strange things in her mouth, I had to taste and see if this really was ice cream.

It was. Vanilla and extra creamy. The cold sweet hit my tongue and wrapped itself around my mouth. It slowly melted and made its way down my throat and into my stomach leaving a cold trail. Ava was a candy gobbler, but my love was ice cream. It could only have been better had it been mint chocolate chip and if Trina had some rainbow sprinkles to go with it.

She looked back and saw me standing there with a silly grin on my face, another large scoop of ice cream dripping between my fingers and more dripping down my chin. I could have eaten half the mountain. The ice cream was that good.

"Your Highness, we must hurry." Trina motioned at the peak of the mountain. "It's not uncommon for snowstorms to hit late afternoon and we don't want to be trapped on the top."

Now I had to worry about monsters and snowstorms? Maybe Trina was right. Maybe we should have gone with the S'more Shores route and taken our chances.

I nodded and then finished eating the ice cream that melted in my hand. "Lead the way."

"From here we have to walk along the snow path and across the cliffs of Popsicle Peak. Be careful because it's icy and very slippery at the top. One wrong step can send you falling off the mountain and all the king's bakers won't be able to put you back together again."

She turned her back to me and started the steep climb. I stepped carefully in each of Trina's footprints, which was easy to do since she was shorter than me. Despite that, she could walk and climb much faster than I could, and it didn't take long until I huffed and puffed while I tried to keep up.

Once in a while, when the slope was extra steep, there were handles attached to the ground to help balance and pull us forward. Luckily for Trina the bars were on her right side so she could use her remaining hand. I still shuddered every time I thought about crushing her hand and wondered how she could act like it was no problem.

We finally reached the path cut into the side of Popsicle Peak. Trina stopped walking and pointed. "This is the only way to get to the other side. When the path narrows when we get to the cliff, keep your back pressed into the mountain. And one more thing. Don't look down no matter what."

I gulped. My legs already felt wobbly from our climb, and I worried I might topple over here on somewhat flat ground. Now she was telling me we would have to walk across a cliff?

Not waiting for me to answer, Trina pushed ahead toward the tallest peak. Although the path started out with a fairly easy climb, it didn't take long for it to become extremely narrow and, at times, seemed to hang in mid-air. Facing outward toward the valley below, we inched along, keeping the icy walls of the peak at our backs. Have I mentioned that I am not a brave person? And I really don't like heights either.

"Has anyone you've known fallen off the mountain?" I couldn't stop myself from asking, although I avoided looking down over the edge of the cliff we were inching across. This probably wasn't the best time to ask a question like that.

"My grandmother's brother fell, but that was way before I was born."

I opened my mouth, but Trina answered my question before I could ask. "No, they couldn't save him. He was just tiny bits and pieces by the time they found him in the valley below."

I wasn't happy. The wind blew stronger with each passing minute. It was obvious we hadn't arrived at the mountain early enough, thanks to our mishap with the Maple Syrup Swamp. Sudden gusts pushed our bodies one way and then another, making us both unbalanced. Plus, it was a freezing wind and my teeth chattered together nonstop. I couldn't feel my fingers and I'm sure my lips had turned blue. Maybe eating all that cold ice cream hadn't been such a good idea. I got to the point where I shook so hard that I could barely put one foot in front of another.

"Trina, can we take a break?" My teeth clacked together and, along with the howling wind, made it almost impossible to hear myself speak.

"There's a cave just ahead. We can stop there for a few minutes."

I nodded and inched along. I couldn't believe they had narrow slippery paths cut into the sides of cliffs with no guardrails, or even ropes, to keep people from falling off.

I had to duck my head to enter the cave, which looked like it had been carved from Popsicle Peak itself. The ice walls were bright yellow and smelled like lemonade. If I hadn't been so freezing cold, I would have tasted it. I shivered, stamped my feet, and rubbed my hands together, trying to get warm.

"Is it always this cold up here?"

"When I've crossed the mountain before with my mother, we always went mid-morning, when there isn't any wind. The sun makes it quite warm so you can sometimes see little waterfalls dripping off the peak." Trina shook her head. "I've never crossed this time of the day. I don't think I want to ever try it again."

"I hope we don't have to come back this way." I wasn't sure I could face enduring the dangerous path a second time.

After a brief rest in the ice cave, which did nothing to warm me up, Trina motioned for me to follow her again. "We're almost to the other side. The Duke should have sleds at the ski entrance. We can use those to get to the bottom of the mountain."

Knowing that the hike was almost over, I inched a little faster and before long, we turned a corner and creamy vanilla ice cream ski slopes welcomed us. Just as Trina had predicted, there were sleds waiting.

"Amber, I don't think I can ride one on my own." She lifted her handless arm. "I won't be able to steer."

I looked at the sleds and then back to her. "I think we can both fit on one together. I'll go in front and steer. You can sit behind me and tell me what to do."

Being from Southern California, Ava and I are more beach girls and warm sun than cold winds and snow girls.

There's a ski resort a few hours from our house, but we'd never been, so I had no idea how to sled. Trina helped me move the toboggan to the top of the slope and I sat in the front. I braced each foot on the narrow platform in front of me as she instructed. Two leather straps, which looked like reins for riding a horse, were mounted on the platform.

Trina gave me a small shove to get us sliding. Before we picked up speed, she jumped on behind me and wrapped her arms around my waist. The smell of cinnamon and cloves tickled my nose and my stomach growled. Trina must have heard the growl because she loosened her grip and leaned away from me.

The sled picked up speed and Trina yelled in my ear. "Use the straps to turn the sled from right to left, then back again. That'll slow us down. We don't want to go straight down all at once. We'll crash at the bottom if we do."

I followed her instructions and sure enough, the sled started slowing. I heard my stomach growl again, but louder. I couldn't believe I was that hungry after eating so much ice cream. It growled again even louder and Trina screamed. I turned my head to look back at her. That's when I discovered it wasn't my stomach that had growled. Instead, a huge white monster chased us, its mouth open in a roar.

Chapter 16

Trina's arms pulled away from my waist and her screams abruptly stopped. Even the growling monster went silent which scared me even more. I glanced back over my shoulder. The gingerbread girl and the monster were nowhere to be seen.

"Trina!" I was horrified I'd let the monster get her.

I tried slowing the sled and hoped I could turn around and rescue her. But the slippery slope was too much for me to handle and the sled slid faster yet. I looked back and hoped to catch a glimpse of Trina. There was nothing but blinding vanilla ice cream. My friend was gone.

The bumpy ride made me turn my attention back to my downhill slide. I couldn't control the speed any longer. The whistling, freezing wind made the tears in my eyes turn to ice crystals and everything went blurry. I fought with the reins as the bottom of the ski run came rushing toward me, but I still couldn't slow down. I thought about throwing myself off the sled then decided that might hurt too much.

As I buzzed past a ski hut, several people came out and chased after me. They yelled for me to stop. I definitely would have stopped had I known how, but since I didn't have Trina giving me directions, it was a lost cause. I pulled back harder on the reins, hoping it would work like a brake. Instead, the sled flew up into the air, a foot or two, then crashed back into the ice cream snow.

I felt like my body moved in slow motion as the sled hit the ice cream and I shut my eyes and held onto the reins as tight as I could. The weight of my body, as it crashed back onto the sled, knocked the air from me. I could barely breathe. But that wasn't what bothered me the most . . . it was the bruise forming on my bottom that was going to make it hard to sit down for days. Somehow, despite going airborne, I'd managed to keep the sled upright and I continued to speed down the slope.

A short distance ahead of me, a grove of pine trees blocked my way. I suddenly realized there was no way I would miss crashing into them, so I threw myself off the sled, and tucked and rolled, like I'd learned in gymnastics. The snow was as hard as I'd imagined and the air was knocked out of my lungs, again. New bruises were added to my body.

There was a deafening crash and bits of brown sugar cone and green icing flew through the air landing around me. I shivered, thinking that could have been me if I hadn't jumped in time.

Rough hands grabbed my shoulders and pulled me to standing. The owner of the hands had a wrinkled face and frizzy white hair. His shoulders were stooped beneath a black sweater which was littered with icing fragments from the demolished trees.

"Are you okay?"

"What were you thinking?"

"Who are you?"

"You could have been hurt!"

Several voices chattered all at once while the old man just stared at my face.

"I think I'm okay, but the snow monster has my friend, Trina. We have to save her!"

I looked at the group that surrounded me. There were regular humans like me, a yellow rabbit, a few gingerbread people, and two marshmallow Peep chicks, who twittered nonstop. No one would look me in the eye, including the old man.

"Isn't there anything we can do to rescue her?" I was ready to fall on my knees and beg for help. "We can't just leave her up there to die."

"I'm sorry, Miss. If the monster has her, she's already gone." The white-haired man took my hand. "I'm sorry about your friend. You must not be from around here, otherwise, you'd have known that."

The group moved in closer to get a better look at me, like I was an oddity on display. Then I remembered I was still covered with swamp goo. The maple syrup had dried, leaving my hair in sticky spikes. Kind of a punk rock look. My clothes and skin were stained a brown color and I smelled super sweet with a slight sulfur odor.

"Um, I fell into Maple Syrup Swamp." I waved my hand up and down my body. "Mister Minty sent me to see the Duke. That's why Trina was with me. She was helping me get here and we ran into all kinds of trouble."

I stopped talking when I realized I was rambling. They still stared at me and didn't say a word. "You see my little sister was kidnapped by Queen Frosting and I was hoping the Duke could help me."

One of the gingerbread men started shaking his head back and forth, muttering under his breath before he turned his back and walked away. I thought I heard him say "Get in line, sister. He's more interested in skiing than helping us."

I looked at the rest of the group who stood around me. "Can any of you tell me where I can find the Duke?"

"Last I heard he was at Bonbon Castle." The old man scratched his head. "Maybe you should clean up and change clothes before you go see him though. He doesn't take kindly to riff-raff off the street."

"How do I get to the castle?"

The yellow rabbit inserted herself in front of the old man. "I'm going there right now, honey. I'll take you."

"Thank you."

"Mistress Buttercup is my name. I'm Mister Minty's niece. What's yours, child?"

"I'm Amber."

"Nice to meet you, Amber." She used her umbrella to move the old man out of her way. "Come along, dear. If my uncle told you to see the Duke, then see the Duke you shall."

"Is Mister Minty at the castle now?" I was anxious to talk to someone who knew who I was and tell him about Trina. Maybe between the green rabbit and the Duke, they would have a plan for saving both Ava and Trina. I refused to believe that Trina was dead.

"Why no, dear. He left on urgent business five days ago and no one has seen or heard from him since."

Chapter 17

"What do you mean no one's seen him?" I was sure he'd planned on meeting the Duke right away. "He left me with the gingerbread people last night to go straight to the Duke's villa."

"That's odd." Mistress Buttercup twitched her whiskers and wrinkled her nose. "The Duke came to the castle this morning throwing a fit and yelling for everyone to find Ambassador Minty."

"All I know is that Mister Periwinkle found us at the Toffee House last night and said the Duke commanded him to come to his villa right away. Rapidamente."

"That sounds like the Duke. Not thinking of the consequences of traveling in the dark in these times."

"Mister Minty took off right away and Mister Periwinkle said he had to warn the people of the kingdom that the evil queen was gathering her forces." I looked at the frightened face of Mistress Buttercup. "They left together, and then Trina and I left when the sun came up. We never saw any signs of Mister Minty."

"Oh dear, I fear something terrible has happened to my uncle." She took my hand and pulled me faster along the road. "Let's get you to the castle and get you cleaned up. The Duke needs to hear about this as quickly as possible."

When we reached the gates of Bonbon Castle, Mistress Buttercup pulled a lace hat from her handbag, placed it between her ears, and then used her paws to smooth her whiskers down. She pushed a button and the ten-foot-tall black licorice gates slowly swung open. The castle was five stories tall and about two football fields long. Sparkling glass windows glittered in the late afternoon sunlight. Gems of every color were embedded in the castle's stone walls and, when the sun hit them just right, colorful rainbows shot out of them.

Mistress Buttercup marched us to the closed entry doors and pressed another button. After waiting a few minutes, she pushed it twice more and I heard her tsking under her breath. When the doors finally opened, an old gray rabbit dipped his head toward us.

"Mistress Buttercup, to what do we owe the pleasure of your visit today?" He put a pair of silver wire glasses on his nose, looked at me then stepped back. "And what do you have here? I can't allow this, this . . . thing in the Duke's castle."

"You do mean King Cookie's castle, don't you Mister Ash?" Mistress Buttercup's ears were twitching faster and faster but before she could get another word out, the gray rabbit interrupted her.

"Ah, that would be Sir Ash to you. Don't forget the Duke bestows honors on those who are most loyal to him." If it were possible, the gray rabbit stuck his nose even further up into the air. "As long as King Cookie abandons his kingdom, this shall be the Duke's castle. He is sacrificing everything to protect this land and its citizens from the evil queen."

"Whatever you say, Sir Ash." She practically hissed as she said his name. "However, this poor girl needs a bath and a place to stay. Mister Minty sent her to see the Duke and it is most urgent."

"So you say, Mistress Buttercup, so you say." He moved closer to me and inspected me from the top of my head to the bottom of my feet, then sniffed. "Wait here. I will see what the Duke wishes to do."

With that, he slammed the door in our faces.

"Is there someone else I can talk to, who might be able to help find my sister and friend? They don't seem to want me here."

"Don't mind Sir Ash. He really should be retired but won't give up his post. Makes him feel important I suppose."

After another few minutes of waiting, the door slowly opened, and Sir Ash stuck his head out of the narrow crack. "Go around the back to the servants' entrance. One of the women will receive you there."

With that, he slammed the door in our face again.

"Well, I never! Come along, Amber." She led me to the back of the castle and pointed out the gardens. "This was Princess Sugarpop's favorite place. All of her lollipop flowers died, and the strawberry fountain dried up after she disappeared."

"Princess Sugarpop rescued Trina and me from Maple Syrup Swamp!" I was happy to pass along some good news.

"Really and truly? She's alive?" A frown creased her forehead. "Why hasn't she come home to rule the kingdom instead of letting the Duke take over?"

"Well . . .." Maybe it wasn't such good news after all. "Apparently her sister turned her into a horse, and she can't come home."

There was a loud gasp beside me and when I looked at Mistress Buttercup, she was pure white. "Oh, that poor child. Cursed to be such a dreadful beast."

"In my land, horses aren't dreadful. In fact, they are very good friends with us."

She gave me a funny look and shook her head. "I think you were in the swamp too long. No more talk about monsters until you meet with the Duke."

A gingerbread woman met us at the servants' entrance and curtseyed to us. She introduced herself as Taffy then poured a cup of hot cider for Mistress Buttercup and placed a plate of chocolate éclairs on the table. Once the rabbit was settled in front of the cozy fireplace, Taffy led me to a small bathroom in the basement. Half the room was taken up by a glass tub already filled with steaming hot water and bubbles.

"Here miss, use this soap. It will remove all traces of maple syrup from you." Her green eyes looked at my sticky and stained torn clothing. "I will find something suitable for you to wear."

Once I had the door locked, I wrestled out of my clothes. Maple syrup is like glue once it dries, and I think I pulled some skin off with my shirt. I was sad to see my Taylor Swift T-shirt get thrown away. It was my only souvenir from the concert my mom took me and Jada to for my eleventh birthday several months ago. But I was realistic. My shirt and shorts would never be clean again.

Dunking myself under the water I started scrubbing with the pink soap. It smelled like cinnamon gummy bears and burned my skin a little bit. But, before long, I was maple syrup free, even my hair.

A soft knock sounded on the door, and it opened a few inches, even though I knew I had locked it before undressing. Taffy placed some folded clothes on a chair. "The Duke would like to see you in fifteen minutes. You should make sure you're ready, Miss. He hates to be kept waiting."

"Thanks, Taffy. I'll be ready."

I dressed as quickly as I could but fumbled with the unfamiliar dress. An underdress of white filmy material went on first, reaching down to my ankles. On top of that, a light pink apron-type dress hung over my shoulders with long ties that wrapped around my waist to hold it in place. The apron reached to my knees and had tiny candy canes and peppermint starlight candies embroidered along the hem. The shoes were similar to what Sir William loaned me. I supposed his shoes had made their way to the same trash bin as my T-shirt and shorts.

I walked back up to the kitchen and tried to dry my hair by the small fireplace. I knew it was hopeless since I had long, thick curly hair. It takes forever to dry even with a blow dryer, which I doubted they had in this kingdom.

Taffy came and pulled on my arm. "The Duke will see you now."

"Are you coming with me, Mistress Buttercup?" I was terrified. I wanted a friend to be there with me when I begged the Duke to save my sister.

"I'm sorry, Amber. You must talk to the Duke on your own. I'll be waiting here for you when you're done."

I nodded and followed Taffy down a long hallway. We reached an arched iron door that was guarded by two men. Two very tall and very wide men. My mom would have called them stocky, and they looked a lot like professional football players. They opened the door and pushed me inside before clanging it shut.

The Duke sat on a golden throne, staring at a huge map covering the wall. I almost couldn't walk forward because I felt like I had looked into a mirror. He had long, curly black hair and his amber eyes were the same color and shape as my own.

Chapter 18

The Duke of Custard didn't look at me, so I took a few steps forward and cleared my throat. Finally, he either heard me or saw me because he waved me forward. I curtsied when I stopped in front of him.

"Well? Who are you and what do you want?" The Duke had an accent that was different from everyone else I had met in this strange land. Maybe it sounded a bit like Italian, but I wasn't sure. The only Italian I'd ever heard was when I'd listened to phrases on Google after I found out my real dad was from Italy.

The Duke had a white cast on his leg and had propped it up on purple pillows. A small circle of gold sat atop his dark curls.

"Um, yes, Your Highness." I hesitated. Were Dukes Highnesses, or Dukenesses, or what? "My name is Amber and Mister Minty suggested I speak with you."

"Yes? Get on with it girl. I've got important business to

attend to." He ran his olive-skinned bejeweled fingers through his thick hair. "And where is Mister Minty, might I ask? He's left me in a lurch taking off like that."

"Mister Minty left the Gingerbread people last night to come to see you. I don't know what happened to him."

His amber eyes narrowed and looked at me closer. "And just what was he doing at the Toffee House? Scheming to turn this kingdom over to the evil queen?"

"No! Nothing like that!" Oh boy, this wasn't going like I had hoped. Before I could stop myself, my words tumbled over each other as they popped out of my mouth. "He rescued my sister and me, but then the evil queen kidnapped my sister. Then Trina helped me come here but we fell into the swamp and then the snow monster took her. I need you to rescue them."

The Duke's loud laugh echoed in the empty throne room. It scared me because it wasn't a happy laugh.

"Mister Minty sent you to ask me to rescue some girls?" The Duke practically spit out the word girls before he scowled at me. "He knows I don't have the time for a ridiculous mission like that. I have a kingdom to protect. Leave me and find them on your own."

He flicked his hand toward the door behind me and picked up some papers. He gazed down at them and ignored me. I hadn't wanted to bring up the Golden One, but he left me no choice.

"Excuse me, Duke?" I hesitated to see if he would look at me. When he didn't, I rushed ahead anyway. "The reason why Mister Minty sent me to ask for your help is that he believes my sister is the Golden One."

I didn't think now was the time to mention that Princess Sugarpop thought I was the Golden One. I was sure I wasn't, and I certainly did not want to be. Better to let people think it was Ava.

"What?" The Duke's voice echoed in the enormous room and his face turned red. "Mister Minty is a bigger fool than I thought. The Golden One is a legend. He or she does not exist. I'm the one who will save the kingdom from this curse."

"But Mister Minty said you sent him to try and find the Golden One." I was confused. I was sure the green rabbit had said the Duke was counting on the Golden One to save them.

"I was trying to get that blasted rabbit out of my hair. He was annoying me with 'Golden One' this and 'Golden One' that." He scowled and threw the paper he'd been reading onto the floor. "It figures that fool would find a child and claim she's The One."

I should have accepted the fact that the Duke of Custard was not going to help me, but I just had to open my big mouth and argue. "My sister, Princess Ava, has strong magic. The evil queen knows she's the Golden One and that's why she took her."

The Duke stood and hopped off the dais, being careful not to bump his broken leg. He came at me faster than I thought he'd be able to move with the cast on. He grabbed my arm and squeezed tight.

"Now listen here, girl. There is no Golden One. I should have you thrown into the dungeon for spreading malicious rumors." He gripped my arm hard enough to make me gasp then released me. "Now get out and don't let me ever see you again."

I finally figured it out. The Duke didn't want to help anyone but himself. With the King and his two princesses out of the way, the Duke had taken over and he didn't want the Golden One to interfere.

I was still worried about being thrown into the dungeon, so I made myself cry. Huge crocodile tears dripped down my cheeks. It was a handy thing to know how to do when I got in trouble and grownups wanted to think I was really sorry.

"I'm sorry, Your Highness." I threw in a hiccup. "I'm just so worried about my little sister I made it all up. Please don't arrest me. I promise I'll leave and never bother you again."

He smiled, not a very nice smile, then hobbled back to his throne. "Good. Don't say another word to anyone about this Golden One. Mister Minty is an old rabbit who is confused. If you run into him, you make sure to tell him he's no longer welcome in my court."

I did a quick curtsy and ran from the throne room. After leaving the two guards behind, I barreled into the kitchen and almost collided with Taffy. She nearly dropped the cup of apple cider that she'd been pouring for Mistress Buttercup. The yellow rabbit must have seen the tears on my cheeks because she hopped up and pulled me into a hug. Her fur smelled like Lemonheads.

"What's wrong child?'

"The Duke is too busy to help me and doesn't believe my message from Mister Minty." I shook my head. "I think the Duke wants to become king."

"Shhh, child. Not here," Mistress Buttercup whispered in my ear, then pulled me to the door. "Thanks for the cider, Taffy."

Once we were out on the street, away from the castle, Mistress Buttercup put her mouth close to my ear. Her whiskers tickled me, and I tried not to giggle.

"Amber, you need to keep dangerous thoughts like that to yourself. Too many ears are listening." She grabbed my hand, looked back at the castle, and shivered. "Now, since you need a place to stay you might as well have my spare room. If my uncle shows up, he'll want to talk to you right away."

"The Duke said Mister Minty was no longer welcome at his court."

"That's not good news. In fact, the situation is even worse than I thought." She hopped forward, yanking me after her. "Come along dear, we have a rescue to plan."

Chapter 19

"You mean you'll help me rescue my sister?" Finally, there was someone who might be able to help me. "What about Trina? Can you rescue her too?"

Mistress Buttercup slowed down and shook her head. "I'm sorry dear, there's nothing we can do for Trina."

"But you will help me find my sister, won't you?"

"That's something you're going to have to do on your own. I will help you get to the path that will take you to the evil queen's castle, but after that, you'll have to figure it out."

"But why can't you take me all the way to the castle?"

"It's not possible. The evil queen has placed a spell on Butterscotch Mountain, and we can't cross it. I think she fears an invasion."

"Then how am I going to get across?"

"You're not from our world. I'm counting on that to

allow you to get through the invisible barrier. Once you do, I have faith you'll be able to figure out how to rescue your sister."

"But I don't know how to save her." Tears rolled down my cheeks. They were the real kind this time. "I don't have magic like Ava and I'm just a kid."

"My uncle seemed to think you were important in this fight against Queen Frosting, which makes me believe you're more powerful than you realize."

"No, you're wrong, Mistress Buttercup. It's my sister that's important. Mister Minty thinks Ava is the Golden One." I wasn't going to tell her what Princess Sugarpop said. It was impossible that I could break evil curses and rescue a kingdom.

"Then there's no time to lose. Come along, dear. It's more imperative than ever that you save your sister."

I had to run to keep up with the yellow rabbit, who hopped down the cobblestone street without looking back to see if I followed. I wasn't used to wearing dresses, especially long dresses, and I tripped several times. After I tripped for the third time and fell, landing on my face, I saw I had ripped the new dress. Blood from my scraped knee trickled down my leg. Mistress Buttercup slowed to a walk.

"I'm sorry my dear. I forget humans are so slow."

We walked in silence for another few minutes, before she stopped in front of a lemon-yellow door tucked into the side of a stone building.

"Here we are." She opened the door and motioned me

inside. "Would you like some lemonade with rock sugar?"

"Just some water would be fine." My teeth had started to ache from all the sugar.

I looked around her small house. All the furniture and decorations were in different shades of yellow, the only exception was a framed photograph of Mister Minty. Mistress Buttercup saw me looking at him.

"My uncle raised me on his own since I was a little bunny."

"What happened to your parents?"

"Maple Syrup Swamp." She went back to being busy in her small kitchen. "You were very fortunate, my dear. No one survives the swamp. Now sit and I'll bandage your scrape."

I sat at her kitchen table, which was a glossy dark-yellow color, the same color as butterscotch button candies. Her chairs were small and low to the ground. My knees almost came up to my chest and I felt like I was in a dollhouse. She cleaned my knee, then spread honey over the scrape and placed a bandage on it.

A knock at the door startled the yellow rabbit and she dropped the pot of honey. Golden sticky goo spread across the floor.

"Oh dear. I am jumpy, aren't I?"

"Don't worry, I'll help you clean it up." I grabbed towels while she answered the door.

"Baker Bob, what a pleasant surprise." She lowered her voice to a hush, then murmured something I couldn't understand.

It sounded like she didn't want him to know I was there. Or maybe she didn't want me to know who was at the door. I wondered if this was the evil queen's Bob. My curiosity got the better of me, so I decided to peek and take a look.

I tiptoed to the kitchen doorway and stuck my head out. A young man stood at Mistress Buttercup's open door. A smudge of white flour dusted his nose. His light blue eyes were similar to Queen Frosting's eyes, and he had the same platinum-blond hair color. The big smile on his face showcased the two dimples in his apple-red cheeks. No wonder the queen had fallen in love with him. Without the flour and the white apron on, he looked like a prince.

"I'm sorry Mistress Buttercup, I didn't realize you had company."

I guess I hadn't done a very good job of being sneaky.

"No worries, Baker Bob. This is Amber, a young friend of ah . . . ah, my uncle."

"Nice to meet you, Amber." He waved at me, and I blushed. "If I would have known you were visiting, I would have brought some of my Grasshopper cookies for you. I make my own Grasshopper mint candies and add them to the icing. I'll bring it over tomorrow."

He made chocolate mint candy and cookies too? I think I might have developed a crush on Baker Bob.

"Thank you, Baker Bob." Mistress Buttercup held up a platter of fat pastries that dripped with icing. "You've brought enough cinnamon rolls here for both of us. I know this is a busy time of year for you, so we'll let you get back to work."

"Oh, it's no trouble at all. I'll drop by on my way home from the bakery tomorrow evening."

"Really, that's not necessary. We may be out visiting friends and I don't know when we'll get home." The rabbit started closing the door. "Thank you again for bringing the rolls."

Before the door fully closed, I heard Bob tell me again it was nice to meet me. I felt my face turn hot again. It was a good thing I hadn't had a chance to say anything. My tongue probably would've gotten all twisted up and he would have thought I was a stupid girl. Just like the Duke thought.

"Oh dear, I had hoped no one would find out that you're staying with me." She bent down to clean up the honey I had forgotten about. "I worry that the Duke will decide you're a threat and throw you in the dungeon after all. Or even worse, the evil queen might send someone after you."

Chapter 20

Mistress Buttercup woke me up while it was still dark. As I put my clothes back on, I found she had mended the rip and shortened the dress while I slept. It hung just above my knees, instead of hitting my ankles. I guess she didn't want me falling on my face today. I met the rabbit by her front door, and she gave me a cinnamon roll to eat along with a small pack filled with candy and water. After she locked her door, I followed her silently through the dark, quiet town. We reached the countryside just as the sun peaked over Butterscotch Mountain.

"We have about another hour before we reach the base of the mountain. Do you need to rest yet?"

"No, I'm okay." I was grateful she'd reduced her pace to fit my slow walk, instead of bounding ahead.

"There are very few people out this way, but we'd better be quiet just the same. No need for anyone to know where you're going."

I nodded and followed behind her on the small path that wound beside a small brook and into patches of forest. I sniffed the air. It smelled like mint. I looked closer at the rectangular leaves hanging off the almost bare branches. They were light green and looked like the gum my dad liked to chew.

"Is that gum?" I asked the rabbit.

"Yes, we're in Spearmint Forest. The trees haven't been happy so I'm afraid it won't be a good harvest year." She pointed up the tall thick trunk. "On normal years the leaves are so thick you can't even see the sky. The Marshmallow Peeps used to nest here but they've had to find new homes. I'm afraid the trees might be dying."

As I followed Mistress Buttercup quietly along the narrow path, I saw her long ears begin to twitch, and then her whiskers started to quiver. She turned and pulled me through bushes and deeper into the forest.

When I opened my mouth to ask what we were doing, she put her paw to my lips and shook her head back and forth. She took my hand and led me into the even thicker brush. Motioning that I should be as quiet as possible, we crept at a snail's pace. It wasn't until we stopped in front of a hollowed-out tree that I heard a horse clip-clopping in the forest. It wasn't the horse that gave me the shivers, but the man's voice calling out my name.

"Amber, I know you're here. Come out, come out wherever you are."

Some people might have thought it could be a nice man trying to help rescue my sister. But, the way the hairs on the back of my neck stuck up and the way Mistress Buttercup's ears trembled, I knew it was someone who shouldn't find us. I had no idea if the evil queen had sent him or the Duke. It didn't matter. It would be bad if either of them captured us.

"We want to help you, Amber." The man's voice sounded closer. "Don't make me waste my time looking for you. Come out, come out!"

The rabbit put her mouth close to my ear. "I'm going to lift you. Climb into the hollowed-out trunk as far as you can go, and you'll find a small hiding place in that large branch on the left. No matter what you hear, stay there until you know it's safe."

I whispered back quietly. "What are you going to do?"

"I'm going to distract him. Hopefully, he'll follow me and leave you alone."

"No! That's too dangerous."

"Don't worry about me, dear. We have to keep you safe." Her yellow eyes twinkled at me. "Besides I'm one of the fastest bunnies in Sweet Treats Kingdom. He's not going to catch me."

As soon as I was hidden inside the narrow, hollowed-out tree branch, I heard her scuttle through the underbrush. Almost immediately, the horse snorted directly below me. My body shivered uncontrollably, and I hoped I wasn't making any noise.

"Amber, I know you're hiding. Let us help you."

I clenched my teeth together to make sure they didn't chatter and held my breath. Just when I thought I might pass out from lack of oxygen, I heard the horse clomp away from my hiding spot. I exhaled as slowly as I could. When I thought the man was far enough away from the hollow tree, I gulped in mouthfuls of air. Trickles of sweat dripped down my face and back.

"I see you, Amber." The man sounded irritated. "Don't make me chase you."

Since his voice had moved further away, I assumed he had spotted Mistress Buttercup. I shivered again as I worried about what would happen if he caught her. I hoped she was right about being the fastest bunny.

While I waited, for what felt like an hour, my foot fell asleep. It made me feel even more miserable. I wanted to shake it and move around but, afraid I might make noise and the man would find me, I didn't move a muscle. As I waited on Mistress Buttercup, I worried about how I could rescue my sister from an evil queen when I couldn't even rescue myself from a regular guy on a horse. Instead, I'd had to rely on a bunny rabbit to save me. Princess Sugarpop was wrong. There was no way I was the Golden One. I might get lucky, though, and could perhaps help Ava escape and find our way home. Most likely I'd fail, and Ava would have to save herself.

I chewed my thumbnails down until they bled. I finally

heard movement in the brush below me and shivered again. Had the man found my hiding spot after all?

"Amber." Mistress Buttercup's quiet voice brought me great relief. "You can come down now."

I poked my head out of the branch and looked down. Her fur was covered with dirt. Sticky spearmint leaves and small sticks were matted on her arms and legs, but she had a smile on her face. I wiggled out as best I could, then fell on top of her. She grunted but stayed standing firm when she caught me. It felt like needles prickled my foot and I shook it trying to get the blood flowing again.

"Oops. Sorry." I kept my voice to a whisper, uncertain we were out of danger. "Are you okay?"

"Yes, but we'd better remain quiet and stick to the forest for the rest of the way."

"What happened to the man?"

"Nothing we need to talk about. It's best we hurry." She pulled me forward. "There may be others looking for you."

Chapter 21

Moving quietly through the forest took extra time but we finally reached the base of Butterscotch Mountain by the time the sun shone directly overhead. Mistress Buttercup had me drink water and eat some candy and honey cakes while she drew a map for me.

"This is as far as I can go. I had hoped you could walk over the mountain, following the path, but I think with people searching for you, you'd better use the tunnel."

"Tunnel? What tunnel?" I shuddered. "Are there bats or rats?"

She gave me a funny look and twitched her nose. "I don't know what those are, so I guess we don't have them."

"What about dragons or monsters hiding in there?" I probably have watched too many scary movies with my friends. It seemed like a fun thing to do at the time but now my imagination wasn't helping my situation.

"Focus, Amber. There's nothing in the tunnels that can hurt you." The rabbit coughed and muttered something about the evil queen that I couldn't understand. "Anyway, this will be much safer than being out in the open where she or the Duke will find you."

"Don't they know about the tunnels?"

"Hard to say. They haven't been used for mining for over fifty years and the entrance is hidden." She pulled an iron key hanging on a rusty chain from her pocket and handed it to me. "My great-great-grandfather owned the mine and when it closed, he locked it. Our family uses it from time to time for picnics and other celebrations."

I thought a tunnel was a strange place for a picnic but then again, all of this land was strange. "What did your family mine for?"

"Butterscotch Buttons, of course."

Of course, that's why it was called Butterscotch Mountain. "Why did you stop mining? Did it run out of Butterscotch Buttons?"

"Unfortunately, it did. Now we have to import them, but with the evil queen's curse the shipments have stopped." She placed the map on the ground. "No more questions. You need to be on your way."

Mistress Buttercup quickly pointed out the small path I needed to take and explained how to open the door and relock it after I was in. She promised me the path through the tunnel was wide open and I wouldn't get lost. I hoped she was right.

"When you reach the end of the tunnel this key will open that door too. Don't forget to lock it on your way out. From there it will take you about an hour to walk to Cinnamon Castle." She looked down at my legs. "Well, maybe it will take you two hours to get there."

"Is that where I'll find my sister? Cinnamon Castle?"

"Yes. The evil queen took it over when Lord Cinnamon didn't return with her father." She frowned. "I suspect Queen Frosting had something to do with the disappearance of the king, but no one has been able to prove anything."

Great, if she could do away with her father and curse her own sister, I didn't stand a chance. I guess I really did love Ava if I was willing to walk straight into danger.

Mistress Buttercream cleared her throat and rattled the paper. I turned my focus back to the map.

"Once I reach the castle, how do I get in?" I was pretty sure I couldn't just walk up to the front door and knock.

"Sneak around to the west side. Use the shrubs and topiaries to hide yourself." She pointed to the west which was a good thing. I had no idea what was east or west here. "There should be trellises for the licorice whips and you can climb up those to reach a window on the second floor. Once you're inside, you'll have to use your best judgment on how to find your sister."

"And once I find her, what should I do?"

"Try to sneak her out the same way you went in and bring her back through the tunnels. I'll wait at the edge of the forest for two days. If you don't return by then, I'll assume you've failed and are a prisoner of the evil queen."

"Okay, I guess I should go now." I picked up the map, which shook in my quivering hands. I wished there was someone else who could rescue my sister. "Thank you for all your help, Mistress Buttercup. I couldn't have gotten this far without you."

She gave me a hug, her fur warm and lemony against my face. "Stay safe, Amber, and bring the Golden One back to us."

I hurried down the path she'd marked on the map and was soon hidden from sight by the huge boulders that littered the mountainside. It didn't take long until I found the moon-shaped rock, and the tiny iron door hidden behind thick spearmint leaf bushes. It was right where she'd said it would be. The key unlocked the door, and it swung open without a sound.

I was relieved that there weren't spider webs hanging over the entrance. That happens all the time in those scary movies, and you just know if there are webs there'll be huge spiders to chase you. I found the lantern hanging right where Mistress Buttercup told me to look and, as soon as I turned it on, pale golden light lit up the trail. I started down the path and then remembered I was supposed to lock the door behind me. I hurried back to the entrance.

Before I put the key into the lock, I heard horse hooves clopping on the stone path.

"I know you're hiding here, Amber." The man's voice was low and sounded like a growl. "You might as well give up since there's nowhere left to hide."

My hands shook and turned sweaty. I barely hung onto the key as I tried to fit it into the lock. This didn't sound like the same man who'd chased us earlier. How many men searched for me and how had he found me? Could he see the door? The key finally slipped into the keyhole, and it turned silently. With the door locked, I ran as fast as I could toward the other side of the mountain.

Chapter 22

I ran until my legs felt like they would give out on me. Thankfully, the path through the mountain was wide and smooth so I didn't have to worry about tripping and falling. I slowed to a walk and tried to catch my breath. Even though I had a stitch in my side, I kept pushing myself to go faster.

The lantern wasn't all that bright, and I almost ran into the door before I saw it. I slid the key in and turned the lock. Once again, the door swung silently open. I peeked out from behind the thick bushes hiding the door and listened. I didn't see anyone who could harm me, nor could I hear anything, except some twittering birds. I carefully stepped out of the tunnel and locked the door behind me.

The tunnel had deposited me about a hundred feet up from the bottom of the mountain and a narrow track led down to a wide valley. Looking across the valley below me, I was surprised at how green the grass and trees were. I guess I expected something snowy or dreary since she was an evil queen. Colorful marshmallow Peeps flitted in and out of the spearmint bushes and their chirping made me feel safer. Wouldn't they be quiet and hide if there was danger heading my way?

Once again, there were large boulders for me to hide behind as I walked down the track. I waited, every so often, to listen for a horse. When I didn't hear any human or horse sounds, I'd continued on, repeating the process every few minutes, until I reached the valley. A small sparkling stream flowed from the base of Butterscotch Mountain and ran toward Cinnamon Castle. Its dark red towers rose in the distance. Seeing the huge fortress where my sister was held made my stomach feel like I'd been on a tilt-a-whirl. I wanted to turn around and run back to Mistress Buttercup. But I couldn't. My sister needed me to rescue her.

With feet that felt as heavy as they'd been after dunking in Maple Syrup Swamp, I started toward the castle. I kept the stream in sight but stayed off the path, relieved there were plenty of trees, large bushes, and tall grass to give me cover. Halfway to the castle, I heard the hooves of a horse running along the path. I dove headfirst into a thick spearmint bush. The Peeps, who had been noisily chirping as I walked, became quiet when the horse slowed to a walk. I heard bushes rattle close to where I hid. My heart began beating so hard that I thought it would burst out of my chest.

"Are you hiding in there, Amber?" It sounded like the

same man from the other side of the mountain. "You can run but you can't hide forever. Come out, come out."

From my hiding spot, I could see he was dressed all in black and wore a hat that resembled an upside-down peanut butter cup on top of his black curly hair that reached to his shoulders. His black mustache and goatee made his amber eyes stand out.

I sucked in a breath, then held it, hoping he hadn't heard me. He looked like the Duke of Custard. Could it be his brother?

"Come out, come out wherever you are." The man's gravelly sing-song voice creeped me out. Did he really think I was that stupid? My fingernails dug into my palms as he stepped closer and closer to my hiding spot. I bit down on my tongue to keep from whimpering. Just when he was a mere two feet away from finding me, several Peeps burst from the bush next to my hiding spot and flew straight at the man. His horse reared up as the creepy guy yelled, and they took off at a run toward the castle. I took a deep breath and tried to still my trembling legs, which felt like cooked spaghetti. I wasn't sure how I'd be able to manage the long trek to the castle.

I crept out from beneath the bush and tried to brush the sticky mint candy that clung to my clothes and hair. I gave up when I hadn't made much progress after several swipes. The Peeps settled back into their nests and resumed their cheerful chirping.

"Thank you for chasing him away," I whispered to the

Peeps as I walked past their bush. "You saved my life."

I have no idea what the Peeps were trying to say but they all started chirping at once. It was hard to believe such tiny birds could make such loud noises. I waved to them and continued on my way to the castle, keeping as far off the path as possible.

I reached the castle grounds without any further trouble. The castle looked huge and I didn't feel capable attempting the rescue on my own. I wished again that either Mistress Buttercup or Mister Minty were there to help. Since I knew I wouldn't be able to win a fight against a powerful, magical queen, I told myself, repeatedly, to be extra sneaky. All I had to do was grab Ava and run. My pep talk didn't help. My legs started quivering again and my heart beat like one of the drums in the 4th of July parade my family attended every year.

The turrets of the castle were red and white twisted columns. They looked like giant hard candy sticks and spicy cinnamon aromas tickled my nose when I brushed against one. The walls of the castle looked like slabs of peppermint bark, alternating stripes of white chocolate and dark chocolate. Peppermint starlight candies were embedded in the chocolates, creating wavy patterns using the red and white round candies.

I didn't see any guards posted on the outside of the castle which relieved me. There weren't many bushes to hide behind. Following the directions Mistress Buttercup had given me, it didn't take long to find the licorice whip trellises.

Using the sticky whips to balance myself, I clumsily climbed the wooden bars and only slipped once. Luckily, I caught myself before falling ten feet down, but several of the licorice whips weren't so fortunate and broke in half. As they broke, the strong smell of black licorice filled the air and my breath caught in my throat. I have never liked the smell or the taste of black licorice since it has always reminded me of icky medicine. Now it would always remind me of being stuck in Maple Syrup Swamp. Not a memory I wanted to ever think about again.

I looked down at the broken whips littering the lawn. So much for being sneaky. If guards patrolled the grounds, they'd know right away someone was breaking into the castle, using the second-floor window. I considered climbing back down and hiding them but decided against it since I'd almost reached the window. It wasn't worth the risk of falling again.

The window slid open easily and I climbed into an empty bedroom. It contained a small bed and table, both covered with white sheets. It appeared the room hadn't been used in a long time because the floor was dusty. I sneezed, then froze, while I listened to see if anyone had heard me. No pounding footsteps headed my way, so I let out the breath I'd been holding.

After wiping my nose on the embroidered apron, I tiptoed to the door, cracked it open, and peeked out. Not seeing anyone, I opened the door and hoped it wouldn't squeak. It didn't. I took a deep breath in and tried to calm my shaking hands. I wasn't sure how much more stress I could manage.

The hallway ran alongside all four outside walls of this part of the castle with doors at regular intervals. It reminded me of a hotel. It was a wide-open space in the middle of the hallways, going from the floor all the way up to the ceiling. There were five floors in all. The walls were red and white striped and soft black carpet covered the floors. It would cover the sounds of my footsteps, making it easier for me to sneak around.

I started for the staircase, which curved from where I stood onto the ground, and stopped, mid-step, when I heard a giggle. I'd know that sound anywhere. It was my sister's giggle. I searched the open floor space below me but didn't see her. I wasn't sure where her voice came from.

"Stop. You're tickling me." Ava laughed louder, and the happy sound echoed off the walls.

I heard someone else laugh but it sounded more like a young girl instead of the queen. Halfway down the stairs, I paused to listen for Ava's voice. She sounded close but I still couldn't see her. I slowly made my way down the remaining stairs, making sure I didn't trip and roll to the bottom as I strained my ears to hear my sister's laugh again. I may be athletic, but I am definitely not graceful . . . and I'm even a klutz at times.

Once I reached the ground level, I found that instead of an open floor plan like the upstairs, there were hallways leading off from the central open space. My mom would have called it an atrium. I heard footsteps marching down one of the corridors coming toward me. I scurried until I reached a huge potted plant sitting at the edge of the open space and crouched behind it.

As the marching boots burst into the room, I saw they belonged to the same man who'd been hunting for me earlier. And he was heading straight for my hiding place.

Chapter 23

Creepy guy had his head down, reading a piece of paper, so he didn't see me. After walking right past me, he entered another corridor. I patted my chest and tried to quiet my heart, which jumped around like a jackrabbit. While I tried to get my hyperventilation under control, I heard Ava and the girl shriek. My heart jumped back into my mouth.

"Where's the queen?" The man's demanding voice echoed down the hallway he had marched through.

"I don't know. She said she was going out for a drive around her kingdom." It was a girl's voice that answered. She sounded older than me, but it was hard to tell because of the way her voice echoed off the slick walls. "Don't sneak up on us like that. It's annoying."

"When will she be back?"

"Raul, I have no idea. My sister doesn't tell me anything."

Could that be Princess Sugarpop with my sister? Maybe she could help us escape since the queen wasn't around to stop us. I only hoped Raul wouldn't stay to wait for the queen's return.

"Yes, Your Highness. Let her know I'll be out searching and will come back later this evening."

I assumed he would be coming back the same way he entered, so I left my hiding place and hid behind a large red and white twisted pillar furthest from the corridor he had taken. Once again, I heard the marching boots coming toward me, echoing in the large open space. I cringed and shut my eyes but at the last moment, instead of reaching my hiding space, the marching steps turned and headed in another direction.

When I could no longer hear him, I snuck a peek around the pillar. With no one in sight, I tiptoed across the open space and headed into the corridor Raul had taken when he'd scared my sister. The hallway spilled into a huge room. Windows, spanning two stories up, covered two walls and looked out onto a colorful flower garden. Rainbow hued butterflies and birds flitted around the blooms. Sunlight flooded the room making Ava's golden hair shine. She sat on the floor and combed Princess Sugarpop's mane. A tangle of bright pink flowers adorned the horse's tail. Ava hummed while she combed Princess Sugarpop, which meant she was happy.

The princess had her long legs tucked beneath her while she ate caramel corn spread onto a mat sitting on the floor in front of her. Her eyes were half-closed as she munched, and she looked content.

Tears stung my eyes. I missed Ava and felt angry with myself for almost never letting her brush and decorate my hair, even when she begged. I couldn't believe how mean I'd been to my little sister, never wanting to play or spend time with her. No wonder she was happier with Princess Sugarpop.

I stepped into the room and prepared myself for Ava's disappointment in my arrival. It was clear to see she was happy here. Instead, she dropped her brush, jumped up, and rushed to my waiting arms.

"Amber, why didn't you come with me? I missed you!" Her tiny body climbed up mine until her arms were wrapped around my neck and her legs were locked around my waist. "Can we go home now?"

Princess Sugarpop scrambled to her feet, or I guess her hooves and bowed before me. "Welcome Golden One. Did you see the Duke? Are you here to break the curse?"

"I am so, so sorry Princess. I don't know how." I hugged Ava even tighter. "I've come to rescue my sister and find a way to take her back home."

The horse's head drooped, and she turned away from me. I knew she'd hoped I would turn her back into a girl and save the kingdom, but I didn't see how that was possible. I had no magical abilities.

"Ava, is your magic strong enough to turn Sugarpop back into the princess?"

"No, silly. I can't do tricks unless Queen Frosting lets me use her wand." My little sister giggled. "She wants me to call her mother but she's not my mom, is she?"

As nice as it was standing here hugging my sister, I knew we had to get out of there before the queen found us.

"Sugarpop, can you help us back to Butterscotch Mountain? If I can get back to Candy Village, I think I can find someone to help us find our way home." I really and truly hoped that would be the case. "Some creepy guys have been chasing me all day long. I think one of them is Raul?"

"Yes, Raul and Rolly." Princess Sugarpop kept her head lowered toward the ground. She wouldn't look at me. "The Queen sent them to find you."

"You mean so she could kill me or curse me or something?" I was terrified Raul, or the queen would return before I had Ava out of there. I knew Rolly was out of the picture, thanks to Mistress Buttercup.

"No! Nothing like that. Princess Ava missed you so much my sister wanted to bring you here to live with us."

Ava nodded. "I missed you, Amber."

"Missed you too, baby." I shifted her weight to my other hip. "Can we leave before Queen Frosting shows up? I don't think she's going to be too happy with me taking Ava away from her."

Freezing cold air hit my body and I shivered.

"No one is going anywhere." Queen Frosting's cold voice made icicles appear in the air.

Chapter 24

I slowly turned around, holding Ava tightly in my arms. The queen stood three feet away from me. Her magic wand pointed at us while snowflakes floated from its tip. I started shivering. Certain death, or at least a curse, was headed my way.

Ava patted my cheek. "Why are you shaking? Are you cold?"

I put Ava down and hid her behind my body. I tried to make my voice strong. "My sister belongs with me. I'm taking her home."

Queen Frosting laughed and, even though I didn't think it possible, the room got colder. "Your sister missed you, but I can tell you're a troublemaker. Perhaps you need a little lesson to teach you to be grateful for everything I'm offering you."

As the queen lifted her wand to curse me, Ava flung herself in front of me. She screeched her high-pitched voice until I thought the windows might shatter, then wrapped her arms around my legs. "No! You can't do that! She's my sister and I love her."

Queen Frosting blew out a breath which sent frosty ice to whiten my black curls. "Well, well. Maybe you both need a lesson, then."

I flung Ava behind me. "No! Don't punish Ava. I'll take whatever curse you want to throw at me, just don't hurt her."

Ava pushed herself back in front of me and stomped her foot. "Don't you hurt my big sister. Punish me instead."

Queen Frosting lowered her wand. "You really love each other so much you'd sacrifice yourself to save your sister?"

Ava and I both nodded and I wrapped my arms around her. I still shook, wondering what would happen to us.

Princess Sugarpop clomped over to her sister and nudged her shoulder. "I'd do the same for you, Frosting."

"Really?"

"Of course! Why do you think I stay here even though everyone else calls you the evil queen? I love you, no matter what."

Tears trickled down the queen's cheek and the room began heating up. She kissed the horse's head. "I thought you stayed because I made you. Aren't you angry with me for turning you into a horse?"

"Well . . .." Sugarpop snorted. "It was fun for a while, but I miss being a girl. Can't you change me back?"

The queen began pacing and snowflakes dripped from her wand. The room plunged into iciness, again.

"What's wrong, Frosting? Can't you fix me?"

"Yes, but I don't think I should until I fix the whole kingdom." She shook her head and frost flew into the air. "I didn't mean for it to get out of control like this. I wanted to fix my mistake before Father came home, but when I couldn't, I had to keep our kingdom sealed off until I can figure it out."

"Father? You mean Father is still alive?" Princess Sugarpop practically pranced.

"Yes, I'm sorry you didn't know. I thought you did."

My head bounced back and forth between the Queen and the horse. I started getting my hopes up that we weren't going to be cursed after all.

"What happened? What do you need to fix before I can turn into a girl again?"

"When Father said I couldn't marry Bob I was so angry. I'm sure you heard my tantrums." The queen smiled then fluttered her wand. The room warmed up again. "When he left to meet that prince, I decided to take matters into my own hands and rule the kingdom. I put a blocking spell in place so they couldn't return until I married Bob. Then it would be too late for Father to do anything about it."

"So, what happened? What went wrong?" I clamped my hand over my mouth. I should probably try to stay quiet and invisible since I wasn't sure we were entirely safe yet.

"Bob turned me down. He said it was dishonorable to go

against Father's wishes and we had to find another way to get his blessing." The queen scowled. "I couldn't bear to be in Bonbon Castle and risk running into Bob. I moved here until I could find a way to change his mind about marrying me. Then the Duke of Custard decided he'd rather rule the kingdom. He planned on kidnapping you, Sugarpop, and forcing you to marry him so he could become king."

"Marry me? But I'm only eighteen!" The horse snorted. "And I don't love him."

"Exactly. I had to protect you and the only way I could think how was to turn you into something. I remembered how much you loved horses."

"What about your monster that ate my friend Trina and her family? How can you say you're trying to save the kingdom when you kill people?" My mouth seemed to run on its own. Otherwise, I would never have brought up the monster. I was asking for trouble by bringing attention to myself.

She didn't say a word but lifted her wand once again. I threw myself in front of Ava and squeezed my eyes shut. I'd finally gotten her angry enough and she was going to curse me after all. Instead, I heard a tinkling bell and then a side door burst open. I could smell the cinnamon before I saw the gingerbread people carrying in trays of cookies and tea.

"Amber!" Trina ran toward me, both hands stretched out. "I was so afraid something bad happened to you."

"Me? The monster grabbed you, not me." I took hold of both her hands. "What happened? How did you get your hand back?"

Trina glanced at the queen, a shy look on her face. "Queen Frosting fixed it. And my arm too."

"But I don't understand. How did you get away from that monster?" I felt more confused with each passing second.

"You mean Marshall?" Queen Frosting laughed. "He's nothing more than a giant marshmallow that's soft and cushiony inside. I sent him to rescue people who were in danger from the Duke. He was supposed to bring both of you here, Amber, but being a marshmallow apparently, he forgot."

Trina must have seen the look on my face. "Really, I'm okay. My mother and aunts are here too."

"Why did Marshall take them?" I had a hard time following this after being convinced Queen Frosting was so evil for so long. Okay, we'd only been in Sweet Treats Kingdom for three days, but it felt like three long years.

"Did you notice that things are dying on the other side of Butterscotch Mountain? That there are very few animals living there and they all live here?" the Queen asked me. "The Duke of Custard has not been a good ruler and in fact, wants the land to fall apart so he can blame me. That way when he declares himself King, he can force the people into a war against me. They'll be on his side because they'll believe I'm evil."

"But what did the gingerbread women have to do with the Duke? Why were they in danger?"

Trina answered this time. "Because the Duke didn't want

our toffee chips harvest to make it to market. He wanted to destroy the gingerbread clan and blame it on the Queen. She's brought as many of my clan as she can to the castle and the others she's turned into horses to keep Sugarpop company."

"I only turn people into horses when they wanted to try it out." She twirled her wand between her fingers. "Some days I'm so busy turning them back and forth I don't have time to do anything else."

"Why did you let Trina and her family believe their mother was dead?" I'd never forget Sir William trying to create a home for the group of ginger boys who'd lost both their mothers and fathers. They had no hope that their family could be alive.

Trina, up until now, had remained silent. She reached over and grasped my arm. "Queen Frosting tried, several times, to send messages to my family. The duke always intercepted them, and her messengers ended up in the dungeon. She had to stop trying."

I gave Trina's hand a squeeze and nodded. It still made me sad for the ginger kids not knowing, for so long, what'd happened to their family. I turned my attention back to the queen. "None of this explains why you kidnapped my little sister and said she's your daughter. Why would you do that and let everyone think you're evil? Everyone is terrified of you."

"The Duke threatened to throw Bob into the dungeon if I tried to exonerate myself. I couldn't risk it." The Queen hung her head. "As for my dear Ava, when she landed here in Sweet Treats Kingdom, I could feel her magic. I knew she belonged with me so I could protect her."

I glared at Queen Frosting. "That still doesn't make a lot of sense. You didn't have to call her your daughter and take her away from me."

"You're right, Amber. I'm sorry. I guess my reasoning was clouded by trying to keep Bob safe. I hoped that when the Duke found out from his spies that I had a daughter, he'd think I'd married someone else and had completely forgotten about Bob." She reached out and placed her hand on my shoulder. It was toasty warm. "Please forgive me. I shouldn't have taken her from you."

I nodded and gave Ava a quick hug.

Princess Sugarpop nudged her sister's shoulder. "Frosting, isn't it time you let your family and friends help you rescue the kingdom? Isn't it time to forgive Father and let him come home?"

Chapter 25

"You're right, Sugarpop. It's time to stop trying to do this on my own." Queen Frosting raised her wand and instead of snowflakes and icicles shooting out, cupcake rainbow sprinkles filled the air, twirled around, and flew out the window. "Father will be here soon."

Ava released my hand and ran to the queen. She wrapped her small arms around the queen's middle and hugged her. "Please fix Princess Sugarpop."

"Of course, my dear." She lifted her wand and instead of rainbow sprinkles shooting out, a cloud of sparkly pink candy glitter swirled around the horse.

Ava clapped her hands and smiled from ear to ear as Princess Sugarpop emerged from the pink glitter. She wore a glittering pink ball gown, and a small circlet of diamonds sat on top of her long platinum-blonde hair. My sister's pink flowers were still entwined in the princess's flowing locks.

Sugarpop ran to her sister, and for several long minutes, they held each other. Ava climbed back into my arms, and I rocked her back and forth. When the glass doors leading to the garden were flung open, the quiet moment was shattered. The King had returned.

Their father was short and bald, but his daughters shared his arctic ice-blue eyes. His face turned red, and his white walrus mustache quivered. He looked mad. I couldn't blame him though, after being blocked from returning home for so long.

He strode into the room and stopped short of his two daughters. He glared at Frosting and crossed his arms in front of his portly chest. She kept her head down and her eyes closed. A tear trickled down her cheek. The king stood there for what seemed forever, not saying a word. Then all of a sudden, he laughed. Not just a social, polite laugh. It was a loud, belly laugh and then he flung his arms wide and pulled both his daughters into a hug and swung them around. Not an easy thing to do since they were both taller than their father.

"Frosting, I should ground you for the rest of your life." His voice sounded like a bellow and then he broke out into another hooting laugh. "But, lucky for you, I'm too happy seeing you both after all this time."

"Father, I'm so sorry I blocked you from coming home. I missed you too!" Frosting smiled, but she didn't seem all that happy. "But I am not marrying that prince."

"You are right, my dear. After spending a few months

with that spoiled brat while trying to find a way around your spell, I packed him up and sent him home." He shook his head. "Nasty young man. I'm sorry I tried to force you to marry him. I've had a lot of time to continue my search and I think I found someone else more suitable for you."

He motioned for the people who were standing outside in the garden to come in. The group was large, and they filled half the enormous room.

"No, please Father, I'd rather not marry." Frosting had tears running down her cheeks. "I can't do it."

"Nonsense, daughter." He handed her a handkerchief and waited until she dried her eyes. "Now be a good girl and put a smile on your face. He's out in the garden waiting to see you."

Princess Frosting took a huge breath, drew herself up to her full height, and pressed her lips together. Her voice turned frosty and the air around us turned cold. "As you wish, King Cookie."

With the sun shining through the glass windows, it was difficult to see the prince that King Cookie had chosen. The only thing I could see was his dazzling blond hair. Frosting screamed and started crying again, before running toward the open glass door. She threw herself into the prince's open arms and kissed his cheek.

I blinked several times, trying to focus my eyes against the glare before I realized it was Baker Bob.

"Attention everyone." King Cookie clapped his hands several times. "I think we have a wedding to plan for sunset tonight. Please see Mister Minty to pick up your list of things that need to be done."

I searched the room and saw the short green rabbit peeking over the shoulders of the taller men who surrounded him. I grabbed Ava's hand and pulled her with me as I ran toward him.

"Mister Minty! Mister Minty!" I yelled to make myself heard over the din of the excited crowd. "I'm so glad you're safe."

He bowed low. "Your Highness. It is a pleasure to see you have broken the evil curse and rescued our kingdom."

"What? We didn't do anything." I looked at Ava who shrugged her shoulders.

"Oh, but you did Golden One." He pointed to me. "Your love and determination to rescue your little sister and even sacrifice yourself, if necessary, overcame the curse."

I smiled and picked Ava up. "Can there be two Golden Ones? Ava was willing to sacrifice herself to save me too."

The rabbit laughed. "Of course, Your Highnesses. You will both be honored at the wedding banquet tonight."

I looked over at the king and Princess Sugarpop deep in conversation. I missed my mom and dad, and I knew Ava did too.

"As much as we'd like to stay for the wedding, isn't there any way we can go home now? Isn't Frosting's magic strong enough to send us back?"

"All in good time my dear, all in good time."

"What about the Duke of Custard? He's still at Bonbon

Castle. We didn't get rid of him." I worried there wouldn't be a happy ending if the Duke started a war.

Chapter 26

Mister Minty's eyes twinkled. "A little birdy told me that as soon as the Duke heard King Cookie had returned, he packed his bags and went on an extended ski vacation. Far, far away."

"That's good news. I don't want to think a war is coming to Sweet Treats Kingdom."

"Not to worry." Mister Minty signaled to someone walking through the glass door. "I'm going to turn you over to my niece, Mistress Buttercup. She'll prepare you for the wedding and banquet."

The yellow rabbit hopped over to us and before she could bow to me, I gave her a hug and introduced her to Ava.

"Your Highness, I am so happy you fulfilled your destiny." She bowed as soon as I had released the hug. "Follow me. I'll show you to your room. There are gowns set out for you and Trina and her mother will arrange your hair and polish your nails."

I looked down at my chewed-up thumbnails, then tucked them beneath my palms. I really didn't want anyone to see my bad habit.

Ava and I followed her through a maze of hallways and climbed three flights of stairs before entering a door. The bedroom was huge and contained two beds covered with white and gold spreads. A crystal chandelier hung from the high ceiling, casting golden light across the room. Trina and her mother stood in a corner. They both curtsied when we entered the room.

Trina ran to me, and we hugged. "Amber isn't this the most exciting thing ever? A royal wedding!"

"Trina, your manners." Her mother curtsied in front of us again and pulled her daughter back. "Princess Amber and Princess Ava, it is an honor to serve you."

"Really, Mrs. William, we're not royalty. Please call us Amber and Ava."

"Then you must call me Therese." She curtseyed again. "Now, let's get you ready for the wedding."

The two gingerbread women brought out two ball gowns from the closet. Ava's gown was sky blue with silver lace trim and my gown was emerald green with gold lace trim.

"Amber, I'm really going to be a princess!" Ava twirled in her new dress while Trina tried to fasten a small diamond tiara on her dancing head. "Do you think I can wear this trick-or-treating when we go home? I know I'll get extra candy for being so pretty."

I couldn't help myself and laughed. "Don't you think you've had enough candy to last a lifetime?"

"Well, maybe for a while," my sister admitted. "I'm kind of hungry for carrots and ranch dressing."

My mouth fell open. The only way Mom could get Ava to eat vegetables was to hide them in food. "I'm sure we can give you some when we go home."

Ava danced her way over to me and raised her arms to be lifted up. Once her arms were circled around my neck she whispered in my ear. "When can we go home? I miss Mom and Dad."

"Soon, Ava. I'll try to figure out a way when the wedding is over." I slid my sister down to the floor.

Once Trina and Therese had styled our hair, curly and pinned high on our heads with our tiaras secured, they led us toward the garden.

"Princess Amber? Might I have a word with you?" Therese had reverted back to being formal. "If you have need of a ladies' maid when you return to your land, Trina would be happy to go with you to serve you and your sister."

"Therese, I would love to take Trina home with us, but really, we aren't royalty. We're just normal girls who go to school and have to do our own chores." I pointed to my ball gown. "We certainly never dress up like this or wear tiaras back home."

"I thought I'd ask. She's getting old enough that she needs to find her own way." She patted my hand. "We'll find something for her."

"Talk to Mistress Buttercup. I'm sure she'll have an idea."

"Thank you, my dear. Now let's get you both to the wedding."

Chapter 27

Lord Cinnamon asked everyone to take a seat in the garden. As soon as the crowd settled, my little sister walked down the aisle as the flower girl. Instead of throwing flowers though, she let sparkling snowflakes float to the ground. When they didn't melt in the warm air, I knew they were magical. Princess Frosting – no longer a queen now that her father, the king, was back –began her slow wedding march down the snowflake-covered aisle. Her wedding dress shimmered with white jewels and more snowflakes. Baker Bob's smile almost split his face in two as he beamed at his bride.

Before Lord Cinnamon introduced the newly married Princess and Prince, Bob placed two plain cupcakes on a tray and Frosting used her wand to send swirls of buttercream piled high on them. They fed each other a cupcake and cheers erupted across the garden. After the introduction, the crowd followed the beautiful bride and handsome prince to the ballroom for dinner. Princess Frosting allowed us to sit at the bridal table and placed Ava next to herself. I sat next to Ava and Princess Sugarpop sat on my other side.

I picked at the sweets placed in front of me and, like Ava, thought carrots sounded pretty good too. "Princess Sugarpop, can I ask you a question?"

"Of course." She answered even though her mouth was full of strawberry Jell-O and whipped cream. Bright red colored her lips when she licked them.

"Until today, Frosting's wand sent out snowflakes or snowball cupcakes and it was always freezing cold around her. Now she has frosting and candy coming from her wand, and everything is warm. How did that happen?"

"Frosting liked the wordplay on her name. You know Frosting is like icing. Then her nickname is Frost, which is cold and icy." Princess Sugarpop's laugh sounded like tinkling wind chimes. "As soon as she heard about Queen Elsa, she decided she wanted to do the cold thing when she was angry."

"Queen Elsa? I haven't met her yet." I searched the crowd below us, looking for a queen.

"She lives in another land. The Marshmallow Peeps brought back her theme song a few years ago." Sugarpop hummed a few bars of the song.

"Oh no! Not that song." I covered my ears just as Ava started singing the words.

"Let it go, let it go . . . ."

"Please stop, I've heard it a million times too many

already." I elbowed Ava's shoulder.

"Frosting loves that song too," Princess Sugarpop said. "Queen Elsa is her inspiration. Anyway, that's why it gets cold when she gets mad."

Our plates were cleared by the gingerbread people and then they wheeled a ten-tier wedding cake into the room. I couldn't believe it was just plain cakes stacked on top of each other. No icing and no decorations. If anything in Sweet Treats Kingdom was going to be covered with candy and frosting, it should have been the wedding cake.

Princess Sugarpop leaned over to me. "Bob baked the cake. I'm sure it's lemon since that's Frosting's favorite. It's going to be so yummy!"

The bride and groom walked to the cake, both holding onto Frosting's wand. I thought it was a strange way to cut the first piece, but then again, as I've said before, everything in this land was strange. Instead of cutting the cake though, white icing flowed from the tip of the wand and began covering the tiers. When swirls and patterns covered each layer, Princess Frosting tapped her wand three times and then pointed it back to the cake. Colorful candies and sparkling flowers flew out and arranged themselves onto the tiers. It was the most beautiful creation I'd ever seen. All of a sudden, I was hungry and wanted to eat a piece . . . or two.

After the bride and groom fed each other a slice, they asked Ava and me to join them. As we walked down the steps from the raised bridal table, I held Ava's hand. The guests became quiet, and all eyes were upon us. I started getting nervous until Ava giggled and did her happy butt dance.

"You're not a loser anymore, Amber," she whispered to me before we reached the bride and groom.

"Thanks, baby."

When we got to the cake table Prince Bob kissed our hands and Princess Frosting kissed our cheeks.

"Ladies and Gentlemen, we would like to introduce the Golden Ones who united our kingdom." Princess Frosting's voice was clear and sweet, unlike the harsh, cold voice she had used when we first arrived in Sweet Treats Kingdom. I liked her better this way. "Princess Amber and Princess Ava!"

The wedding guests clapped and a few whistled. The thunderous noise lasted a long time, and I blushed while Ava's smile beamed across her face. She always did like to be the center of attention. As soon as it quieted down, Frosting took each of our hands.

"The citizens of Sweet Treats Kingdom are eternally grateful, and you will hold a place of honor at our banquet table for all time." Princess Frosting kissed each of us again while the crowd clapped. "Unfortunately for us, Princess Amber and Princess Ava have requested permission to leave and return to their own land. We will miss them and will count the days until they visit us again."

Ava looked up at Princess Frosting. "You mean we can go home now?"

"Yes, sweetheart. If you're ready to go, you can." Princess Frosting kissed Ava again.

"Thank you, Your Highness. We're ready to go home."

I felt tears sting my eyes. I knew I had missed my mom but finally realized that I missed Dad just as much, even if he wasn't my real dad. He still loved me and made me feel a part of the family even though I looked different. He made me feel safe and secure and I knew he would search for me just as much as he would search for Ava.

"Please come back to visit any time you want." Princess Sugarpop had joined us and gave us both a hug. After she kissed our cheeks, she placed a gold necklace that held a tiny candy cane charm around our necks. "Here's something to remember us by."

Princess Frosting held out her wand and then nodded to Princess Sugarpop, who held out her giant candy cane. They encircled us, weaving their magic, and before I could blink Ava and I were falling and spinning in darkness.

Chapter 28

Ava and I landed on our couch, back in our own home, with a thump. Our heads bumped together.

"Ouch." I rubbed my head.

Before I could check on Ava, she'd jumped up and ran through the house. "Mom! Dad! Amber and I are princesses! Look at my awesome princess dress. Amber rescued me and saved the kingdom. She's a hero!"

I smiled. Maybe Ava had grown up a little during our adventure. She'd actually given me the credit.

"Mom? Dad?" Ava's voice sounded quivery. "Are you home?"

Our parents didn't answer. Maybe they were out hunting for us? I looked around the room and saw the Sweet Treats game board sat on the carpet, whole again, and the pieces set up ready to play. Broken glass, from the shattered photo, still littered the dining room floor. The shards glittered in the chandelier light. It was dark outside and the clock in the kitchen told me it was after nine.

"Where's Mom and Dad?" Her voice shook and her blue eyes filled with tears.

"Baby, they'll be here soon. They're probably out trying to find us." I decided I needed to distract Ava from missing our parents. "Let's play another game of Sweet Treats and you can tell me your favorite part of our adventure. I'll even let you have some Gummy Bears if you beat me again."

I knew it was real because Ava and I still wore our ball gowns and the candy cane necklaces hung around our necks. On the fall through the darkness though, our hair had come down and we had lost our tiaras and shoes. Before we could start the game, the front door opened. Mom and Dad rushed in, their arms opened wide.

"Girls, are you okay? We didn't realize the earthquake was centered right here." Mom kissed Ava's cheek and Dad held me in a tight, tight hug. "We barely felt it in Long Beach but heard on the radio how terrible it was here."

"We're okay, Mom," I said as Dad released me before Mom pulled me into a hug.

"Mom! Dad! We had an awesome time in Sweet Treats Kingdom. We're princesses there and Amber rescued me and saved the kingdom." Ava did her happy butt dance and sang at the top of her lungs. "I'm a princess, I'm a princess."

My mom looked us up and down when she finally noticed our ball gowns. "I see you found your Halloween costumes. I wanted to surprise you, but that was quick thinking Amber, making up stories to distract your sister from the earthquake."

"But . . .." Before I could finish my sentence, my dad interrupted.

"I'm very proud of you Amber." He hugged me again and this time I hugged him back as hard as I could.

A Surprise!

I've created a layered bar cookie that is easy enough for young children to help assemble and can be made to accommodate a variety of food allergies. Enjoy my version of a visit to S'mores Shores!

S'mores Shores Cookie Bars

Where the chocolate river meets the graham cracker sand

Ingredients
- 1 cup graham cracker crumbs—either Honey Maid or gluten-free graham cracker crumbs such as Kinnikinnick brand
- 1/4 teaspoon salt
- 1-1/4 cups mini marshmallows
- 3/4 cup chocolate chips (milk, semi-sweet or dark) or gluten-free, vegan chocolate chips such as Enjoy Life brand

1/2 cup walnuts (you can use your favorite nut, or omit it for those with nut allergies.)

1/2 stick (2 ounces) butter or vegan buttery sticks such as Earth Balance brand

1/4 cup light brown sugar

Instructions
1. Preheat the oven to 350 degrees (F).
2. Coat an 8 × 8-inch square glass baking dish with nonstick cooking spray or line with parchment paper.
3. Mix the graham cracker crumbs with the salt and press into the bottom of the baking dish.
4. Layer the marshmallows on top of the graham cracker crumbs (you can use a bit more if you need to fill in any blank areas on top of the crumbs).
5. Sprinkle your choice of chocolate chips over the marshmallows then top with your choice of nuts. My favorite nut happens to be walnuts followed closely by pecans.
6. Place the butter and brown sugar (it's okay if the sugar is hard and lumpy) in a microwave-safe measuring cup and cover with a paper towel. A grown-up should heat the mixture on high for one minute, stirring at the 30-second mark. Heat in additional 20-second intervals until brown sugar is dissolved in the butter.
7. After spooning the butter and sugar mixture over the layers of yumminess, gently press down on the ingredients with the back of a large spoon. You don't need to compact it too much, just a bit.
8. A grown-up should place the baking dish on the middle rack of your 350 degree (F) preheated oven. Bake for 12 to 14 minutes. The bits of marshmallows that show should get golden brown, but not dark. Remove from oven and completely cool. I couldn't

wait to try them, so I placed my dish in the refrigerator for an hour.
9. Once completely cool, cut into 12 to 16 pieces and serve. These are very rich. Small pieces are probably better so people won't feel quite so guilty going back for seconds . . . or thirds . . ..

Acknowledgments

I must first thank my granddaughter, Emory. Without too much complaining, she indulged my attempts at getting her interested in reading during her elementary school years when she'd rather be dancing or playing. Thank you for brainstorming characters and fantasy lands with me, and for patiently reading each chapter with suggestions on what you'd like to see happen next. I will always treasure those days we spent together working on this first book. Thank you to my husband, Dan, for reading and keeping a sharp eye out for those pesky typos and punctuation errors. I owe my beta readers my gratitude for your input in making the book better or letting me know you couldn't put it down: Gay Toltl Kinman, Kathy Keith, and Emory's friends, Tess B. and Tess R.

Without the editing talent of Elizabeth Constantineau of TouchPoint Press, my book wouldn't be nearly as polished and I'm grateful to her for making it the best it could be. And many thanks to
Sheri Williams for believing in my story and making it a reality.

Made in the USA
Columbia, SC
09 February 2024